J. D. Salinger's *The Catcher in the Rye*

J. D. Salinger's *The Catcher in the Rye* (1951) is a twentieth-century classic. Despite being one of the most frequently banned books in America, generations of readers have identified with the narrator, Holden Caulfield, an angry young man who articulates the confusion, cynicism and vulnerability of adolescence with humour and sincerity.

This guide to Salinger's provocative novel offers:

- an accessible introduction to the text and contexts of *The Catcher in the Rye*;
- a critical history, surveying the many interpretations of the text from publication to the present;
- a selection of new critical essays on the *The Catcher in the Rye* by Sally Robinson, Renée R. Curry, Pia Livia Hekanaho, Denis Jonnes and Clive Baldwin, providing a range of perspectives on the novel and extending the coverage of key critical approaches identified in the survey section;
- cross-references between sections of the guide, in order to suggest links between texts, contexts and criticism;
- suggestions for further reading.

Part of the *Routledge Guides to Literature* series, this volume is essential reading for all those beginning detailed study of *The Catcher in the Rye* and seeking not only a guide to the novel but also a way through the wealth of contextual and critical material that surrounds Salinger's text.

Sarah Graham is a lecturer in American Literature at the University of Leicester. She is particularly interested in twentieth-century American novels and poetry, especially in relation to gender, sexuality and trauma theory.

Routledge Guides to Literature

Editorial Advisory Board: Richard Bradford (University of Ulster at Coleraine), Shirley Chew (University of Leeds), Mick Gidley (University of Leeds), Jan Jedrzejewski (University of Ulster at Coleraine), Ed Larrissy (University of Leeds), Duncan Wu (St. Catherine's College, University of Oxford)

Routledge Guides to Literature offer clear introductions to the most widely studied authors and texts.

Each book engages with texts, contexts and criticism, highlighting the range of critical views and contextual factors that need to be taken into consideration in advanced studies of literary works. The series encourages informed but independent readings of texts by ranging as widely as possible across the contextual and critical issues relevant to the works examined, rather than presenting a single interpretaion. Alongside general guides to texts and authors, the series includes 'Sourcebooks', which allow access to reprinted contextual and critical materials as well as annotated extracts of primary text.

Already available:*

Geoffrey Chaucer by Gillian Rudd
Ben Jonson by James Loxley
William Shakespeare's The Merchant of Venice: A Sourcebook edited by
   S. P. Cerasano
William Shakespeare's King Lear: A Sourcebook edited by Grace Ioppolo
William Shakespeare's Othello: A Sourcebook edited by Andrew Hadfield
William Shakespeare's Macbeth: A Sourcebook edited by Alexander Leggatt
William Shakespeare's Hamlet: A Sourcebook edited by Sean McEvoy
John Milton by Richard Bradford
John Milton's Paradise Lost: A Sourcebook edited by Margaret Kean
Alexander Pope by Paul Baines
Mary Wollstonecraft's A Vindication of the Rights of Woman: A Sourcebook
   edited by Adriana Craciun
Jonathan Swift's Gulliver's Travels: A Sourcebook edited by Roger D. Lund
Jane Austen by Robert P. Irvine
Jane Austen's Emma: A Sourcebook edited by Paula Byrne
Jane Austen's Pride and Prejudice: A Sourcebook edited by Robert Morrison
Byron, by Caroline Franklin
Mary Shelley's Frankenstein: A Sourcebook edited by Timothy Morton
The Poems of John Keats: A Sourcebook edited by John Strachan
The Poems of Gerard Manley Hopkins: A Sourcebook Edited by Alice Jenkins
Charles Dickens's David Copperfield: A Sourcebook edited by Richard J. Dunn
Charles Dickens's Bleak House: A Sourcebook edited by Janice M. Allan
Charles Dickens's Oliver Twist: A Sourcebook edited by Juliet John

---

* Some titles in this series were first published in the Routledge Literary Sourcebooks series, edited by Duncan Wu, or the Complete Critical Guide to Literature series, edited by Jan Jedrzejewski and Richard Bradford.

J. D. Salinger's *The Catcher in the Rye*

Sarah Graham

Routledge
Taylor & Francis Group

LONDON AND NEW YORK

First published 2007
by Routledge
2 Park Square, Milton Park, Abingdon, Oxon OX14 4RN

Simultaneously published in the USA and Canada
by Routledge
270 Madison Ave, New York, NY 10016

Routledge is an imprint of the Taylor & Francis Group, an informa business

© 2007 Sarah Graham

Typeset in Sabon and Gill Sans by RefineCatch Limited, Bungay, Suffolk
Printed and bound in Great Britain by
Antony Rowe Ltd, Chippenham, Wiltshire

British Library Cataloguing in Publication Data
A catalogue record for this book is available from the British Library.

Library of Congress Cataloging in Publication Data
Graham, Sarah.
    J.D. Salinger's The catcher in the rye / Sarah Graham.
       p. cm. — (Routledge guides to literature)
    Includes bibliographical references.
    1. Salinger, J. D. (Jerome David), 1919– Catcher in the rye. 2. Caulfield, Holden (Fictitious
character) 3. Runaway teenagers in literature. 4. Teenage boys in literature. I. Title.
    PS3537.A426C327 2006
    813'.54—dc22
                                                                        2006022256

ISBN 10: 0–415–34452–2 (hbk)
ISBN 10: 0–415–34453–0 (pbk)
ISBN 10: 0–203–49601–9 (ebk)

ISBN 13: 978–0–415–34452–4 (hbk)
ISBN 13: 978–0–415–34453–1 (pbk)
ISBN 13: 978–0–415–49601–5 (ebk)

Contents

Acknowledgements

I would like to express my gratitude for the professional and personal support I have received during the completion of this study. First, the research leave awarded to me by University of Leicester in 2005 enabled me to make substantial progress with the project. I would also like to thank the publisher for efficiency and friendly advice, especially Polly Dodson. I am very grateful to the academics who contributed excellent essays to the study, responded to ideas with enthusiasm and met deadlines with unfailing good humour: warmest thanks to Sally Robinson, Renée R. Curry, Pia Livia Hekanaho, Denis Jonnes and Clive Baldwin. In addition, I would like to thank my colleagues in the Department of English and the Centre for American Studies at the University of Leicester for their support and advice, especially Emma Parker and George Lewis. The opportunity to discuss *The Catcher in the Rye* with students in recent years has also been invaluable.

This book is dedicated with love to my parents.

Notes and references

Primary text

Unless otherwise stated, all references to the primary text are taken from *The Catcher in the Rye*, J. D. Salinger (London: Penguin, 1994). The initial reference will contain full bibliographic details and all subsequent references will be in parentheses in the body of the text, stating the chapter and page number, e.g. (Ch. 1, p. 1). The chapter number is provided to help anyone reading an edition of the novel that differs from this one.

Secondary text

References to any secondary material can be found in the footnotes. The first reference will contain full bibliographic details, and each subsequent reference to the same text will contain the author's surname, title and page number.

Footnotes

All footnotes that are not by the author of this volume will identify the source in square brackets, e.g., '[Baldwin's note]'.

Cross-referencing

Cross-referencing between sections is a feature of each volume in the Routledge Guides to Literature series. Cross-references appear in brackets and include section titles as well as the relevant page numbers in bold type, e.g., '(see Texts and contexts, **pp. 10–12**)'.

Abbreviations

All references to *The Catcher in the Rye* after the first reference in each chapter employ the abbreviation *Catcher*.

Introduction

The Catcher in the Rye by J. D. Salinger, published in 1951, is one of the most popular novels of the twentieth century. It has never been out of print, has sold millions of copies worldwide and has been translated into more than thirty languages. A 1998 poll by the Board of the Modern Library places *Catcher* at Number 64 in its list of the 100 best novels in English, while its companion readers' poll places the novel at Number 19.[1] In 2003 the BBC's 'Big Read' campaign ranked *Catcher* at Number 15 in a nationwide poll of favourite novels.[2]

The plot of the novel is relatively simple. It is written in the first person, narrated by sixteen-year-old Holden Caulfield. He has been expelled from his school, Pencey Prep, just before the Christmas holidays for 'flunking everything else except English'.[3] Instead of returning immediately to his family in Manhattan, he decides to spend a few days in a hotel in the city. The novel follows Holden from Saturday to Monday, as he encounters many different people and considers his past, especially the death of his younger brother, Allie. The title of the novel refers to Holden's fantasy of being 'the catcher in the rye and all', a protector of children that he imagines playing in a field of rye near 'the edge of some crazy cliff' (Ch. 22, p. 156). Holden's relationship with Phoebe, his ten-year-old sister, is central to the novel, which ends with Holden sitting in the rain watching her ride a carrousel. The whole text is narrated retrospectively from some kind of institution in California where Holden has gone to 'take it easy' (Ch. 1, p. 1) and is full of memorable phrases, poignant scenes, comedy and anxiety. Its language, themes and style have been hugely influential and Holden Caulfield has become an iconic fictional character, emblematic of troubled youth.

When it was published, *Catcher* received both praise and criticism. The novel was condemned by some readers for its use of expletives and for presenting as a hero an adolescent who drinks, smokes and engages a prostitute. It would be easy to attribute the negative responses of some critics to the social climate of post-war America, a conservative period in which the disruptive potential of teenagers was

---

1   See <http://www.randomhouse.com/modernlibrary/100bestnovels.html>.
2   See <http://www.bbc.co.uk/arts/bigread/vote/>.
3   J. D. Salinger, *The Catcher in the Rye*, London: Penguin, 1994, Ch. 2, p. 10. All further quotations from the novel will be referenced in brackets within the text and page numbers will refer to this edition.

a major anxiety. However, the American Library Association ranks *Catcher* at Number 13 in its list of the '100 Most Frequently Challenged Books of 1990–2000' and also as one of the ten most frequently challenged books of 2005 on the basis of its 'sexual content [and] offensive language'.[4] 'Challenged' means that an attempt has been made to remove a text from a library or school and, indeed, *Catcher* is still regularly withdrawn from high-school reading lists in the USA in response to complaints. Nevertheless, the novel has now sold more than 60 million copies, suggesting that Holden Caulfield is a figure whose experiences reflect something important that resonates with the lives of readers in many different times and places. Surveying material on the Internet shows that *Catcher* continues to be discovered by new readers every year, many of whom want to testify to the significance of a novel written before their parents were born.

This new study of *Catcher* has been written to aid and encourage readers interested in the novel. It is divided into three main sections. The first, Text and contexts (**pp. 1–34**), includes information about J. D. Salinger's career and other fiction; it also contextualises the novel by discussing the character of post-war American society, and then explores the novel itself in detail, commenting on language, themes, structure and key incidents. The second section, Critical history (**pp. 35–66**), surveys the most notable, interesting and provocative essays written about *Catcher*, from the earliest reviews to the most recent analyses: from comparisons with *Huckleberry Finn* (1885) to psychoanalysis, from the characteristics of Holden's 'voice' to the significance of his red hunting hat.

The third section, Critical readings (**pp. 67–118**), presents five essays about the novel specially commissioned for this study that bring *Catcher* criticism into the twenty-first century. Sally Robinson ('Masculine protest in *The Catcher in the Rye*', **pp. 69–76**) discusses 1950s models of masculinity and considers Holden, a young man attempting to shape his male identity, in relation to these. Renée R. Curry ('Holden Caulfield is not a person of colour', **pp. 77–88**) explores the novel's representation of race, especially the ways in which Holden understands his own white racial identity. Pia Livia Hekanaho ('Queering *Catcher*: flits, straights, and other morons', **pp. 89–97**) uses queer theory to consider Holden's confusion about sexual identity in a new light. Denis Jonnes ('Trauma, mourning and self-(re)fashioning in *The Catcher in the Rye*', **pp. 98–108**) employs trauma theory to offer a reading of the novel that suggests that Holden is deeply scarred by Allie's death in a way that shapes everything he does. Clive Baldwin ('Digressing from the point: Holden Caulfield's women', **pp. 109–18**) discusses Holden's reactions to the female characters in the novel and considers what those responses reveal about him. Each essay is prefaced with an introduction that outlines its key concepts and links it to relevant sections of the study. All of these readings apply contemporary literary and cultural theory to the novel with great skill and clarity to create fascinating and innovative insights into the novel.

At the end of the study, there are suggestions for further reading that will support extended research. These include details of other fiction by Salinger that will be enjoyed by anyone who likes *Catcher*, biographies of the famously reclusive author, texts concerned with the culture and society of post-war America,

---

4   See <http://www.ala.org/ala/oif/bannedbooksweek/bbwlinks/100mostfrequently.htm>.

recommended anthologies of criticism of *Catcher* and some of the best web-based resources.

Above all, the aim of this study is to help the reader find her or his own pathway through one of the most engaging novels ever written, by offering a range of information and ideas about this extraordinary text. In the novel's first sentence Holden tells us, 'I don't feel like going into it, if you want to know the truth'. There is no single 'truth' about *The Catcher in the Rye*, but many readers certainly 'feel like going into it' and this study will help them to do just that.

1

Text and contexts

The Catcher in the Rye is one of the most famous novels written in the United States of America in the twentieth century. With sales of more than 60 million copies, it has made Holden Caulfield famous to generations of readers and made a reluctant star of Jerome David Salinger. This chapter begins with Salinger's career, exploring his writing technique and principal concerns, and making connections between *Catcher* and his other works of fiction. The chapter goes on to place *Catcher* into its original context of post-war America, by considering the political and social character of the 1940s and 1950s. It also discusses the controversy that still surrounds *Catcher* in the USA, where it has consistently achieved the status of being simultaneously one of America's best-loved and most-frequently banned novels. Finally, the chapter offers a detailed reading of the whole novel, discussing its structure, characters, language and themes.

Salinger: life and works

Salinger was born on 1 January 1919 in New York City. His father, Solomon ('Sol'), was Jewish and his mother, Miriam, was Christian. Miriam had changed her name from Marie to appease Sol's family. Salinger includes a version of this situation in *Catcher*: Holden remarks that his 'parents are different religions' (Ch. 14, p. 90) and explains that 'my father *was* a Catholic once. He quit, though, when he married my mother' (Ch. 15, p. 101). Salinger had an older sister, Doris; the family lived in Manhattan and Sol had a successful career working for a company that imported luxury foods from Europe. When Salinger (then known to his family as 'Sonny') was thirteen, Sol enrolled him in a private school in New York, McBurney. There is a brief reference to the school in *Catcher*: when Holden loses the Pencey fencing team's equipment, they are scheduled to compete with McBurney (Ch. 1, p. 3). A detail like this encourages the reader to make connections between Salinger and Holden that are interesting, but may be misleading: *Catcher* may reflect some of Salinger's experiences, but it is not an autobiography. Salinger's grades were so poor that he was asked to leave McBurney after two years; his final report from the school summed him up: 'Ability: plenty.

Industry: did not know the word.'[1] Like Holden, Salinger 'got the ax' from school (Ch. 1, p. 3).

Salinger was then enrolled at Valley Forge Military Academy in Pennsylvania where, amongst greater achievements, he lost the Valley Forge fencing team's equipment on the subway.[2] He graduated with a respectable record in 1936, and travelled to Europe to learn aspects of his father's importing business, but his aim was always to be a writer. He decided to go to college, eventually enrolling in an evening class in creative writing at Columbia University in 1939. This class was run by Whit Burnett, the editor of *Story*, the magazine that would be the first to publish Salinger's work: 'The Young Folks' (1940), a description of a party featuring characters who are bored and do not like each other much. Over the next two years, Salinger's short stories were published in major magazines, and in 1941 Salinger wrote to a friend that he was also working on a novel, 'a portrait of himself when young' that would become *Catcher*.[3] In fact, a story in which Holden Caulfield appears, 'Slight Rebellion off Madison' was accepted by *The New Yorker* in 1941, though it did not appear in print until 1946.

Salinger had attempted to enlist in the US Army in 1941, but had been rejected; however, when the United States entered the Second World War, Salinger found that he was now eligible for the draft and in April 1942, at the age of twenty-three, he began his army service. Many of the stories that Salinger wrote during this period were concerned with the war and army life. Typical of these is 'Death of a Dogface' (1944), which disparages the lies told by the war films that Hollywood was then producing. The soldier Philly Burns tells his wife that the problem with Hollywood's version of war is that: 'You see a lot of real handsome guys always getting shot pretty neat, right where it don't spoil their looks none, and they always got plenty of time, before they croak, to give their love to some doll back home.'[4]

By contrast, Philly tells his wife, a real war death is more like that experienced by his sergeant (the 'dogface' of the title) who died an ugly, painful death 'all by himself, and he didn't have no messages to give to no girl or nobody'.[5] Although *Catcher* is very different from this story in terms of its subject matter, there are important similarities. Like Philly, Holden disparages the tendency of Hollywood films to distort the realities of experience. When Maurice (the 'elevator guy' and pimp) punches him, Holden copes by acting like a character in a film, as if he's been shot in the stomach: 'I sort of started pretending I had a bullet in my guts. [. . .] Now I was on the way to the bathroom to get a good shot of bourbon or something to help me steady my nerves and help me *really* go into action' (Ch. 14, p. 93). Although his fantasy distracts Holden from his fear and pain, he recognises that the capacity of film to distort real experience is dangerous: 'The goddam movies. They can ruin you. I'm not kidding' (Ch. 14, p. 94).

In early 1944, Staff Sergeant Salinger was transferred to England, in preparation

1   Paul Alexander, *Salinger: A Biography*, Los Angeles, Calif.: Renaissance Books, 1999, p. 38.
2   Margaret A. Salinger, *Dream Catcher: A Memoir*, London: Scribner/Simon & Schuster, 2001, p. 33.
3   Ian Hamilton, *In Search of J. D. Salinger*, London: Bloomsbury, 1998, p. 66.
4   J. D. Salinger, 'Soft-Boiled Sergeant' ('Death of a Dogface') *Saturday Evening Post* 216, 15 April 1944, p. 18.
5   Salinger, 'Soft-Boiled Sergeant', p. 85.

for the planned Allied attack on occupied Europe in June, known as 'D-Day', in which he participated. Despite his army duties, he continued to write, and the division between his fiction and his own experiences becomes increasingly blurred. For example, in 'The Last Day of the Last Furlough' (1944), the main character is a soldier just about to be posted overseas. Although the protagonist's name is John 'Babe' Gladwaller, he has the same rank and army serial number as Salinger. Before Babe leaves he meets up with a friend, Vincent Caulfield, who tells him that his brother Holden has been reported missing in action. Salinger is overtly placing himself into his fiction (giving his army number to Babe) while creating one of the families that would dominate his writing in the future. Salinger's use of his cast of characters (usually of the Caulfield or Glass families) is not always consistent between texts: Holden Caulfield in *Catcher* is too young to have fought in the war and does not have a brother called Vincent.

From D-Day until the end of the war, Salinger saw a great deal of heavy fighting in France and Germany. The trauma of his experiences is hinted at in his stories, especially 'A Perfect Day for Bananafish' (1948), in which Seymour Glass – a war veteran – kills himself, and in the story 'A Boy in France' (1945) in which Babe Gladwaller struggles to survive on a filthy battlefield. One of Salinger's most famous stories, 'For Esmé – With Love and Squalor' (1950), features 'Sergeant X', who participates in the D-Day landings and is deeply disturbed by his experiences of combat. Some time after the German surrender, Salinger was admitted to hospital for 'battle fatigue'; Sergeant X and Sergeant Salinger seem to have much in common.

When Salinger returned to the USA he brought with him his wife, a European woman named Sylvia; Salinger's biographer describes her as French, but Salinger's sister remembered her as *very* German.[6] In any case, the marriage lasted only a few months. The war continued to reverberate in Salinger's fiction: in the story 'The Stranger' (1945), Babe Gladwaller makes it home alive, but Vincent Caulfield has been killed. Like Holden in *Catcher*, Babe has a beloved ten-year-old sister, Mattie; as they walk home through the Manhattan streets, Mattie takes Babe's hand and asks him a question:

'Are you glad to be home?'
'Yes, baby.'
'Ow! You're hurting my hand.'[7]

All of Babe's frustration and pain about the war is communicated in his physical response to Mattie's question, an unconscious reaction that undermines his positive words. What Babe actually does to Mattie's hand is not described, an effective and recurring strategy of Salinger's writing, which uses inference skilfully and avoids telling the reader how to interpret the text. Equally, the reverse strategy is used for comic effect in *Catcher*, when Holden explains something quite obvious: ' "Lift up, willya? You're on my towel," Stradlater said. I was sitting on his stupid towel' (Ch. 4, p. 27).

In *Catcher*, devices such as leaving certain things unsaid or ambiguous, using

6 Salinger, *Dream Catcher*, p. 71.
7 J. D. Salinger, 'The Stranger', *Collier's* 116, 1 December 1945, p. 77.

language that evokes the intimacy and informality of speech rather than writing, or offering details that contradict Holden's descriptions, are all central to the richness of the novel. These techniques allow readers to make their own decisions about what Holden is really feeling or doing, offering an interpretive freedom that is usually very difficult to achieve in a first-person narrative, especially one that is overtly addressing 'you'. A prime example of this is in the scene with Mr Antolini, when Holden wakes up to find that his ex-teacher is 'sort of petting me or patting me on the goddam head' (Ch. 24, p. 172). After he has left Antolini's apartment, Holden wonders if his interpretation of events (that the teacher was making a 'flitty pass' at him) was correct (Ch. 25, p. 175). The reader is similarly uncertain: despite the dominance of Holden's perspective, Salinger frees, or even forces, the reader to make her or his own decisions about what Antolini's intentions might have been; there is, after all, a difference between sexual 'petting' and friendly 'patting', and Holden does not know which word to use.

Salinger's last published story of 1945 was 'I'm Crazy', narrated by Holden Caulfield. It begins with Holden visiting his teacher, Mr Spencer, the night he leaves 'Pentey' Prep and much of the scene survives into *Catcher* unchanged. Overall, however, it is less comic than in the novel: Holden pities Spencer more overtly, and his reflections on his own situation are less subtle ('I wasn't saying much that I wanted to say. I never do. I'm crazy. No kidding'), disallowing that freedom for reader interpretation that characterises the novel.[8] Comparing the two also shows how Salinger's style sharpens in *Catcher*. In the story, 'Old Spencer handled my exam paper as though it were something catching that he had to handle for the good of science or something, like Pasteur or one of those guys'.[9] In the novel, Spencer simply 'started handling my exam paper like it was a turd or something' (Ch. 2, p. 10), which is more vivid and succinct.

Similarly, the rest of the story lacks the light touch of *Catcher*. Holden goes home and talks to his sisters, Phoebe and Viola: Phoebe is much as she is in *Catcher* and Viola is a toddler with a craving for olives. Both of them, says Holden, are 'one of us' although it is not clear whether the 'us' is the Caulfield family or a like-minded community that includes the reader.[10] Holden and Phoebe have a compressed version of the conversation they share in the novel but without any of Holden's digressions about James Castle or his wish to be the catcher in the rye. The story ends:

> I lay awake for a pretty long time, feeling lousy. I knew everybody was right and I was wrong. I knew that I wasn't going to be one of those successful guys, [. . .] that I wasn't going back to school again ever, that I wouldn't like working in an office. I started wondering again where the ducks in Central Park went when the lagoon was frozen over, and finally I went to sleep.[11]

The story is much more conclusive about Holden's future than the novel and

8 J. D. Salinger, 'I'm Crazy', *Collier's* 116, 22 December 1945, p. 48.
9 Salinger, 'I'm Crazy', p. 48.
10 Salinger, 'I'm Crazy', p. 48.
11 Salinger, 'I'm Crazy', p. 51.

much less optimistic; he is sadly resigned to moving into the adult world of work and already believes himself to be a failure.

'Slight Rebellion off Madison' was finally published in *The New Yorker* in December 1946, five years after the magazine had purchased it. Written in the third person, the story concerns Holden's date with Sally. As in the novel, Holden expresses his hatred for school, which Sally doesn't understand, and he suggests that they run away together, which she declines to do. The story is concise and, like all of Salinger's work, dominated by dialogue. What description there is tends to be comic, as when Holden's dancing style is described as 'long, slow side steps back and forth, as though he were dancing over an open manhole', a perspective on Holden that the first-person form of *Catcher* does not allow.[12] Despite the omniscient narrator, the story has much in common with the novel, sharing its tendency to shift unexpectedly from humour into pathos. Here, as in 'I'm Crazy' and *Catcher*, Holden can be funny, angry and sad in the space of a few short scenes. These rapid shifts in mood can leave the reader in a state of uncertainty that may mirror Holden's own instability.

Meantime, the novel about Holden remained unfinished and Salinger seems to have had doubts about his capacity to complete it. He described himself in 1945 as 'a dash man not a miler' – a short-story writer rather than a novelist – and said it was 'probable that I will never write a novel'.[13] Around this time, plans were being made for a collection of Salinger's stories but Salinger seems to have decided against the idea and, indeed, has never given permission for twenty-one of his early stories to be anthologised, including the Gladwaller and Caulfield stories discussed here. When a publisher reprinted and sold the stories as an unauthorised collection in 1974, the author filed a civil law suit against him. In a rare comment to a journalist at that time, Salinger said that he had blocked publication of the stories because he 'wanted them to die a perfectly natural death'.[14] However, Salinger did allow a selection of his post-war stories (most of which first appeared in *The New Yorker*) to be published together as *Nine Stories* (1953), including such key works as 'For Esmé – With Love and Squalor', 'A Perfect Day for Bananafish' and 'Uncle Wiggily in Connecticut'. The latter was made into a film, released in 1949 under the title *My Foolish Heart*. The film bore little relation to the original story: according to the *New York Times*, the film 'dishes up sentiment by the bowlful' and Salinger hated it.[15] This unhappy experience probably guaranteed that none of his other works would ever be made available for adaptation.

By 1950 Salinger had completed *The Catcher in the Rye* and Little, Brown agreed to publish it in July 1951. Salinger was reluctant to engage in publicity activities, but there was significant interest in the novel anyway: *Catcher* was reviewed in newspapers and magazines across the USA and was generally well received (see Critical history, **pp. 37–40**). It was selected as the Book-of-the-Month Club's choice for summer 1951, a situation that guaranteed publicity and sales. It was

12 J. D. Salinger, 'Slight Rebellion off Madison', *New Yorker* 22, 21 December 1946, p. 82.
13 Hamilton, *In Search of J. D. Salinger*, p. 94.
14 Lacey Fosburgh, 'J. D. Salinger Speaks about His Silence', *The New York Times*, 3 November 1974, <http://www.nytimes.com/books/98/09/13/specials/salinger-speaks.html?_r=1&oref=slogin>.
15 Bosley Crowther, 'My Foolish Heart', *The New York Times Review*, 20 January 1950, <http://movies2.nytimes.com/gst/movies/movie.html?v_id=103324>.

originally published in a bright jacket with an image of a carrousel horse and an author photograph, which Salinger insisted be removed for the reprinted edition. Although it was not the best-selling novel of 1951, it stayed on the *New York Times* best-seller list for the rest of the year.

It is likely that Salinger did not anticipate just how successful his novel would be. In February 1952 he commented that he was 'relieved that the season for success of [*Catcher*] is over. I enjoyed a small part of it, but most of it I found hectic and professionally and personally demoralising.'[16] Of course, the novel continued to sell and by the late 1950s it was being assigned to university courses and discussed by literary critics. It is probable that the interest in Salinger that was sparked by the success of *Catcher* played a significant role in his retreat, first into seclusion (when he moved away from New York to a plain farmhouse in Cornish, New Hampshire, where he has lived ever since) and then into silence (when he ceased to publish his work after 1965). The simple covers on his books are his choice, as if he wants nothing – no image, no author photograph – to distract readers from the content. Although he did publish five long stories (see Further reading, **p. 121**) after *Catcher*, the frequency decreased dramatically; his final publication, 'Hapworth 16, 1924' (1965) was his first new work for six years. In 1970 he repaid the advance that his publisher had given him after his last book, *Franny and Zooey* (a reprint of two stories) and was free of any further obligation to produce work for publication.

Since then, communications from and about Salinger have been rare. He gave his last interview in 1953, to a girl from a high school local to his new home; he married Claire Douglas in 1955 and they had a daughter (Margaret, born in 1955) and a son (Matthew, born in 1960). Margaret's memoir, *Dream Catcher* (2000), offers fascinating insights into Salinger as a writer and a person. In 1967 his marriage to Claire ended in divorce. Salinger had a relationship in 1972–3 with Joyce Maynard, an eighteen-year-old undergraduate, who eventually published a memoir of her time with him, *At Home in the World* (1998). Since the late 1980s Salinger has been married to Colleen O'Neill, about whom very little is known. Throughout this time Salinger has lived in reclusion which, as his daughter Margaret attests, 'doesn't mean that you have stopped entertaining formally; it means that you do not lay eyes on a living soul'.[17] Many anecdotal reports suggest that Salinger has continued to write, but it seems unlikely that he will publish any of his work. In 1974 he asserted: 'I love to write. But I write just for myself and my own pleasure. [. . .] I don't necessarily intend to publish posthumously, [. . .] but I do like to write for myself.'[18] While most authors write in the hope of being published and gaining a readership, Salinger has experienced fame that few other writers have known and has rejected it.

Salinger told Joyce Maynard: 'The minute you publish a book, you'd better understand, it's out of your hands. In come the reviewers, aiming to make a name for themselves by destroying your own.'[19] *The Catcher in the Rye* went out of

16 Hamilton, *In Search of J. D. Salinger*, p. 121.
17 Salinger, *Dream Catcher*, p. 92.
18 Fosburgh, 'J. D. Salinger Speaks'.
19 Joyce Maynard, *At Home in the World*, London: Doubleday, 1998, p. 158.

Salinger's hands in 1951 and it has been reviewed and discussed by thousands of people since then, but there is little sign that Salinger's name has been destroyed. Clearly, there are echoes of *Catcher*, in terms of style and content, in the stories that preceded it. However, the place and time in which Salinger lived and into which his novel arrived is also relevant to any interpretation of *Catcher*. The next part of this chapter will explore the society and culture of the USA in the 1940s and 1950s to contextualise the novel.

Post-war America: society and culture

To understand something of post-war America, it is necessary to look a little further back. The period from the Wall Street Crash of 1929, when the US stock market collapsed, until the beginning of the Second World War in 1939 was known as the Great Depression, an economic crisis that threw millions of people into poverty. The Second World War was an unparalleled horror, and the USA had hoped it could avoid becoming involved. Anxious about the rise of Communism, keen to limit immigration, and resistant to a European influence on American identity, the USA was happy to stay isolated from the rest of the world. However, the Japanese attack on Pearl Harbor on 7 December 1941 killed more than 2,400 American service people and civilians. By 11 December the USA was at war with Japan, Germany and Italy.

The war brought tremendous changes to the USA: there were some shortages, especially of cars and certain luxuries – the slogan of the time was 'Use it up, wear it out, make do or do without' – but for most Americans not actually engaged in the fighting, the standard of living improved dramatically as food production and manufacturing output soared and wages rose.[20] The war pulled the USA out of the Depression: instead of a shortage of jobs there was now a shortage of people to do all the necessary work. In 1940, 9 million people were unemployed; three years later, fewer than 1 million. As more men went overseas to fight (15 million were conscripted or volunteered), more women had to enter the workplace; they constituted one third of the workforce by 1943, although they were almost always paid less than their male counterparts. By 1945, 24 per cent of married women were employed which, given that 80 per cent of Americans during the Depression had opposed the idea of married women working outside the home, signals a significant change in attitudes about women's roles.[21] Six million women (of a female population at that time of 66 million) entered the American workforce during the war, and although women were encouraged to return to the home when the war was over, many enjoyed the opportunity to have a role outside the family and make money of their own. Unsurprisingly, a significant number of women sought further employment in the continued economic boom of post-war America.

After D-Day in June 1944, Allied progress towards victory was relatively quick and 'VE' ('Victory in Europe') Day was declared on 8 May 1945. However,

---

20 George Brown Tindall and David E. Shi, *America: A Narrative History*, 4th edn, New York: Norton, 1996, p. 1238.
21 Tindall and Shi, *America: A Narrative History*, p. 1242.

America's war against Japan continued in the Pacific and was costing thousands of lives on both sides, so a new strategy was deployed: the atomic bomb, first tested at Los Alamos in New Mexico on 16 July 1945. The impact of the atomic bomb would prove to be devastating, not only for Japan, which suffered the loss of thousands of lives when the cities of Hiroshima and Nagasaki were bombed by the USA in August 1945 (forcing Japan's surrender) but also for the world, which had come to the end of the worst conventional war in history only to find itself entering the perilous atomic age. When Holden comments, 'I'm sort of glad they've got the atomic bomb invented. If there's ever another war, I'm going to sit right the hell on top of it. I'll volunteer for it, I swear to God I will' (Ch. 18, p. 127), the novel reveals its awareness of the atomic anxiety of the post-war years. *Time* magazine commented on the global implications of the bombing: 'With the controlled splitting of the atom, humanity, already profoundly perplexed and disunified, was brought inescapably into a new age in which all thoughts and things were split – and far from controlled.'[22]

One estimate suggests that the USA lost around 400,000 lives in the war, most of them in battle. Tragic as that figure is, it is important to understand it in relation to the general losses suffered around the world. Around 35 million people died in the Second World War, about half of them civilians. The physical fabric of the countries in which the war was fought was destroyed by the conflict; millions of people were wounded, homeless and severely traumatised. Because the USA had not experienced this kind of devastation, it was in many respects the most powerful country in the world in 1945. Its only serious rival, so recently its ally, was the Soviet Union (USSR). In the years following the war America was dominated by two issues: the possible spread of Communism from the USSR and the fear that the Soviets would develop and use atomic weapons. These anxieties would shape American politics, society and culture for many years.

The American economy was founded on capitalist principles, meaning that individuals or companies own the means of production and employ a workforce. Soviet Communism, a state-run, rather than privately owned economic system in which, ideally, the workforce owns the means of production, thus presented a challenge to the values of capitalism. Communist allegiance was therefore 'un-American' and so the 'Cold War' between America and the USSR began; rather than physical combat, this was a 'war of ideas and ideologies, of psychology and propaganda'.[23] A key figure in the early years of the Cold War was Senator Joseph McCarthy, who came to prominence in 1950 by claiming that Communist sympathisers were undermining the US State Department. The HUAC (House Un-American Activities Committee) had been in pursuit of 'subversives' since the war began; the combination of McCarthy and HUAC helped to fuel anti-Communist hysteria that led to the persecution of hundreds of people in America. From government employees to Hollywood actors and directors, the HUAC's targets were asked to confess their allegiance to Communism and 'name names', that is, to indicate other people they knew to be 'guilty' of Communism. Those

---

22 'The Bomb', *Time*, 20 August 1945, p. 19.
23 Lary May (ed.), *Recasting America: Culture and Politics in the Age of Cold War*, Chicago, Ill.: Chicago University Press, 1989, p. 82.

found guilty or who refused to cooperate risked being blacklisted; many suffered this fate and their careers were ruined.

McCarthy's so-called 'witch hunts' were the inspiration for Arthur Miller's play *The Crucible* (1953), which uses the trials of those accused of witchcraft in Salem, Massachusetts in 1692 as a metaphor for events in post-war America. McCarthy was successful because he was manipulating a society that had been made self-protective and anxious by the war and was fearful about what might come next. McCarthy was described at the time as a man who 'lies with wild abandon, [. . .] without evident fear [. . .] vividly and with bold imagination [. . .] often with very little pretense of telling the truth'.[24] It is tempting to imagine that Salinger is commenting on McCarthy's activities when he creates Holden Caulfield, who consistently maintains, 'I'm the most terrific liar you ever saw in your life' (Ch. 3, p. 14). However, although Holden does fabricate some bold untruths, not least in Chapter 8 when he talks to Mrs Morrow on the train home from Pencey and tells her that he has a 'tiny little tumor on the brain' (Ch. 8, p. 51), his lies are not intended to harm, and the reader never doubts his sincerity on important issues. By contrast, Carl Luce, Holden's student adviser from his previous school, is an interesting character to consider in the context of the McCarthy era. Many of McCarthy's targets were homosexual men: McCarthy's persecution of them under the guise of anti-Communism concealed homophobia (fear or hatred of gay people) in an era when homosexuality was illegal and socially unacceptable to many people. Holden tells us that 'Old Luce knew who every flit and Lesbian in the United States was. All you had to do was mention somebody – *any*body – and old Luce'd tell you if he was a flit or not' (Ch. 19, p. 129). Luce seems to be a McCarthyesque figure, the holder of secret, shameful information; he is also, like some of McCarthy's victims, able and willing to 'name names'.

The 'pervasive atmosphere of suspicion, self-doubt and fear' in the post-war years was bound to have an impact on the lives of ordinary Americans.[25] Anxieties about the 'Red Menace' (Communism) and the dangers of atomic weapons were only one aspect of a society that was changing very rapidly. A range of factors provoked this transformation: one of the most important was the continuing growth in American economic prosperity after the war. Many people now wanted to own their homes and start families: the increased wealth in the nation meant that many of them could afford to buy, and federal government supported building companies in the creation of huge housing developments outside major cities. Thirteen million new homes were built in the USA between 1950 and 1960; 11 million of these were in the new suburbs.[26] The most famous of these was the first Levittown, built in Long Island in 1947: more than 10,000 identical two-bedroom houses sold to young buyers, the first of many such developments. The suburbs were booming and were predominantly white: Levitt homes were only for sale to white people. When the economic boom of post-war America is cited, what is indicated is the increasing prosperity of the white population, not of all Americans.

24 Tindall and Shi, *America: A Narrative History*, p. 1322.
25 Maldwyn A. Jones, *The Limits of Liberty: American History 1607–1980*, Oxford: Oxford University Press, 1983, p. 530.
26 William H. Chafe, *The Unfinished Journey: America Since World War II*, Oxford: Oxford University Press, 2003, p. 112.

Holden is a city dweller, plainly a part of Manhattan's elite class who, untouched by urban deprivation, would not wish to swap the city for the suburbs. However, the new suburban middle class found that life became easier all the time: 'The Great American Boom is on', declared the financial magazine *Fortune* in 1946.[27] With domestic oil keeping petrol prices low and with car production soaring, the two-car family was not unusual: one for the commute to the city job, the other for domestic use. For the first time, cars became status symbols rather than functional objects, becoming bigger and more luxurious every year. Side effects of the relocation from city dwelling to the suburbs included the appearance of fast-food restaurants to feed people on the move: in 1948 McDonald's, still a family firm at the time, cut its menu to a few key items and introduced paper cups and plates. Drive-in movie theatres and chains of motels begin to appear across the country. All of these developments indicated a population that was mobile and affluent in a way it had never been before.

Life in suburban communities, coupled with the greater leisure time provided by a shorter working week, encouraged new forms of social activities and an increase in church-going. Some commentators wondered whether religious observance that was based on socialising was sincere: believing in God was fine, but Houston Smith contended that more often 'people believe in believing in Him'.[28] The resurgence of practising Christianity in this period is a good example of the intermeshing of politics and social change: government was keen to encourage church-going because, as FBI Chief J. Edgar Hoover contended, 'Communists are anti-God', referring to the Soviet Union's political principle of atheism.[29] President Eisenhower affirmed this: 'Recognition of the Supreme Being is the first, most basic, expression of Americanism. Without God, there could be no American form of government, nor American way of life.'[30] So a Sunday morning at church became a pro-American act, as was capitalism, in which ordinary Americans participated through work and consumerism. It is no coincidence that the motto 'In God We Trust', which had been stamped on American coins since the Civil War (1861–5) was added to American paper currency in 1957. Holden's comments about Christianity suggest that he recognises its dominance in American culture, but he is not prepared to accept its doctrines without thought. In a conservative era, asking questions about the value of religious observance is a significant challenge, and the doubts Holden expresses (at the start of Chapter 14, for example) are an insight into his intelligence and his rebellious character.

The post-war era was one which encouraged consumer spending as never before and consumer credit rose to accommodate the desire to buy. Stephanie Coontz reports that, in the five years following end of the war, spending on food rose 33 per cent, on clothing 20 per cent and on purchases of household goods 240 per cent.[31] Shopping became a leisure activity for ordinary people in the

27 Tindall and Shi, *America: A Narrative History*, p. 1326.
28 Chafe, *The Unfinished Journey*, p. 116.
29 Tindall and Shi, *America: A Narrative History*, p. 1341.
30 Andrew Wilson, *Beautiful Shadow*, London: Bloomsbury, 2004, p. 220.
31 Stephanie Coontz, *The Way We Never Were: American Families and the Nostalgia Trap*, New York: Basic Books, 1992, p. 25.

1950s: shopping malls popped up all over the country and advertising became an industry in its own right, especially once the new marketing domain of television became available. Seven thousand Americans had television sets in 1947; 7 million in 1950; by 1956, two-thirds of the population owned a set, and television viewing became a nightly family ritual.[32] *Catcher* makes clear that Holden lives a very comfortable life in material terms and so there is little sense in the novel that life is changing rapidly for the average American. After the deprivations of the Depression and the war, America was becoming comfortable and materialistic, at least for those in the white, educated, middle class.

The experience of black Americans in this period was very different. The NAACP (National Association for the Advancement of Colored People) had been founded in 1909 to campaign for improved rights of all kinds for African Americans and during the 1930s it focused on the inequalities embedded in the 'separate but equal' principle. This concept, upheld by law, was a cornerstone of segregation: while it claimed to offer white and black Americans the same services, it meant in practice that the facilities offered to black Americans were much poorer than those available to whites. As with so many aspects of American society, the war brought change: around 3 million African Americans served in the forces and the need for workers at home encouraged the desegregation of the defence industries. The migration north and west of black Americans from the southern states revived with the promise of work and, potentially, better treatment. Such changes encouraged black people to become more politicised and so the experience of the war years aided the development of the civil rights movement. This would become increasingly active in the 1950s, not least with the campaigning that resulted in the decision known as *Brown* vs. *Board of Education* (1954) that the 'separate but equal' doctrine had 'no place' in public education.[33] However, desegregation met with intense opposition, and the majority of schools in the southern states remained all-white in the mid-1950s. The Montgomery bus boycott of 1956, triggered by the refusal of Rosa Parks to give her seat on a bus to a white man, brought Martin Luther King Jr. to national prominence as a figurehead in the growing civil rights movement. Action against discrimination and segregation would continue throughout the 1950s and 1960s and often met with violent resistance, especially in the south, but the increased visibility and political power of African Americans from the 1950s onward was a development that could be stalled but not reversed.

Gender roles also changed in post-war America. Although many women who had started work during the war decided to stay in employment, the vast majority returned to the home and were encouraged by government and social pressures to do so. This ethos continued throughout the 1950s: in 1956, *Life* magazine assured readers that 'of all the accomplishments of the American woman the one she brings off with the most spectacular success is having babies'.[34] Men needed jobs to go to when they returned from the war, so women were not desirable in the workplace. Marriage increased and divorce fell; by 1950 almost 60 per cent of

---

32 Chafe, *The Unfinished Journey*, p. 123.
33 Michael J. Klarman, *From Jim Crow to Civil Rights: The Supreme Court and the Struggle for Racial Equality*, Oxford: Oxford University Press, 2004, see especially pp. 292–312.
34 Tindall and Shi, *America: A Narrative History*, p. 1339.

women aged between eighteen and twenty-four were married, 20 per cent more than in 1940, suggesting that young marriage was increasingly the norm. The birth rate soared, adding 30 million to the population of the USA by the end of the 1950s.[35] This was the 'baby boom' that would lead to an unusually large group of adolescents and students in the late 1950s and 1960s, many of whom demanded new ways of living that challenged the values of their parents, producing the so-called 'generation gap'. Holden recognises the conventions that govern his society and usually conforms to them, but at the same time his disillusionment with the adult world anticipates the adolescent rebellions of a later period.

The post-war suburban family was built on a template that provided and promoted different, separate roles for men and women, especially after marriage. Typically, men left their homes each morning to work in office jobs, returning home in the early evening; women stayed at home all day, looking after the children and maintaining the household, reliant on their husbands' income. In the new social climate of the 1940s and 1950s, this model was seen as the ideal, especially for women. In 1945 *House Beautiful* magazine told women that their task was to create the home that their husbands wanted: back from the war, he was 'head man again' and women should 'forget [their] own preferences'.[36] A best-selling book in 1947 was *Modern Woman: The Lost Sex* which suggested that there was scientific proof that 'women could achieve fulfilment *only* by accepting their natural functions as wives and mothers'.[37] In this analysis, an 'independent woman' was 'a contradiction in terms', meaning that a woman who was independent was not really a woman at all.[38] Holden's girlfriend, Sally, fits this model of femininity: she may be at school, but she anticipates having a stable married life – rather than a career – in the near future.

In 1948 Alfred Kinsey published his ground-breaking study, *Sexual Behaviour in the Human Male*; the book was widely criticised for suggesting that male sexuality was more complex and diverse than social standards would have admitted. The study went into its sixth reprint ten days after publication, suggesting a great general interest in the subject of sex and probably in relationships and gender difference too, subjects that people found difficult to discuss openly. Kinsey's equivalent study of women, published in 1953, sold equally well, although it was – not surprisingly in the inhibited climate of the 1950s – even more disparaged for its supposedly immoral untruths about female sexuality than the study of men had been. The dominant social norms of heterosexuality and marriage were not only repressive, but actually antagonistic to gay and lesbian people in this era: Elaine Tyler May observes 'increasing persecution' of gays and lesbians from the war years into the post-war period, despite Kinsey's recognition of the prevalence of same-sex desire.[39] Thus, Holden's confusion and anxieties about sex are very typical of the era in which he lives; many people lived in a state of ignorance about sexual matters and considered their own feelings shameful.

35 Chafe, *The Unfinished Journey*, p. 118.
36 Tindall and Shi, *America: A Narrative History*, p. 1340.
37 Tindall and Shi, *America: A Narrative History*, p. 1340.
38 Chafe, *The Unfinished Journey*, p. 119.
39 Elaine Tyler May, *Homeward Bound: American Families in the Cold War Era*, New York: Basic Books, 1999, p. 63.

Post-war America was paradoxical in many ways. William Chafe confirms that 'family life, particularly in suburbia, was far more complicated and tension-filled than the stereotypes of the fifties would have us believe'.[40] Domesticity was promoted as an ideal for women and many women were perfectly content with marriage and children, but a significant number were dissatisfied. In 1963 Betty Friedan published her study of women of the 1950s, *The Feminine Mystique*, which controversially suggested that many middle-class, often college-educated, women with children suffered from a 'problem that has no name': a profound sense of unhappiness about their role in life, without a clearly identifiable source.[41] The 'feminine mystique' of Friedan's title refers to the unique fulfilment that women were supposed to find in domesticity. Many of the women in Friedan's study were frustrated and disappointed with lives that contained the things that were supposed to make them happy – husbands, children, fitted kitchens – but left them feeling empty. The steep rise in the prescribing of tranquillizers in the 1950s, principally to women, is indicative of a culture that treated unhappiness as an illness rather than the product of oppressive social standards.

Also countering the ideal of domestic bliss is the fact that women did continue to enter the workplace, a change that the increase in 'white-collar' (administrative rather than physical) work encouraged. Even so, a career was no guarantee of contentment for women or men, since the world of work tended to be as rule-bound as home and family. The 1950s is a contradictory period in which conformity is seen both as positive (because it signifies a unified nation with shared values) and negative (because it suppresses individuality). A letter to Betty Friedan in 1964 suggested that 'what is wrong with the women trapped in the Feminine Mystique is what's wrong with men trapped in the Rat Race [. . .] there isn't enough meaningful creative work for *anyone* these days'.[42] The frantic scramble for success in business, termed the 'rat race', could indeed be seen as the male equivalent of women's imprisonment in domesticity. This is reflected in a key novel of the era, *The Man in the Grey Flannel Suit* by Sloan Wilson (1955), in which a model American couple attain everything that the age recommends – steady income, home, children – but remain profoundly dissatisfied, trapped within the roles imposed upon them by society.

David Halberstam describes post-war America as 'a corporate culture in which the individual was *always* subordinated to the corporate good and in which a certain anonymity was increasingly valued'.[43] Social studies of the impact on Americans of the post-war way of life were very popular and abundant in the 1950s; one of the most famous was David Riesman's *The Lonely Crowd* (1950) which asserted that modern, corporate America was not just dull in the conformity it demanded of its male employees, but actually damaging, since it eroded the confidence and self-reliance that were considered positive, even necessary, masculine characteristics. In 1956 William A. Whyte published his critique of conformity, *The Organization Man*, which identified the 'social ethic' of the time as one that prioritised the group over the individual to the extent that the

---

40 Chafe, *The Unfinished Journey*, p. 122.
41 Tyler May, *Homeward Bound*, p. 187.
42 Tyler May, *Homeward Bound*, pp. 190–1.
43 David Halberstam, *The Fifties*, New York: Fawcett Books, 1993, p. 124.

individual actually felt worthless outside the group context. It is clear throughout *Catcher* that Holden recognises the demands that post-war society makes on men and women, forcing them to be 'phony': to compete with one another, be status-conscious and judge success in limited, material ways. Although Holden is principally defined as an adolescent coping with grief and the trials of growing up, his scathing comments about the flaws he perceives in the dominant ideologies of his society – and the limitations they impose upon him as an individual – make him a much more challenging, even subversive, figure than the stereotypical teenage rebel.

The 'teen-ager' was, in fact, first identified as a recognised developmental period and a social phenomenon in the 1950s. Increased affluence, wider inclusion in high-school education, even the greater mobility afforded by the boom in car ownership, combined to create a 'peer culture' (that is, one in which young people refer to each other for a sense of belonging and shared values, rather than to the older generation) such as had never been seen before. As young people spent a significant amount of time – both in school and out – with each other rather than within the family unit, so leisure products and services created with teenagers specifically in mind became a growth industry. In order to express their sense of difference from the world created by their parents, adolescents required films, music, clothes, books and innumerable other products that were designed especially for them. Diners and drive-in movie theatres became places in which teenagers could interact, exchanging ideas and exploring the possibilities of relationships. Such freedoms, especially in a repressive era, caused anxiety about the disruptive potential of adolescents, and social commentators produced many studies of this new sector of society, some promoting understanding, others more inclined to scaremongering about 'juvenile delinquents'. *Rebel without a Cause*, the study of a 'criminal psychopath' written by Robert Lindner in 1944, would give its title (but little of its content) to the iconic film of 1955 that made James Dean the visual representation of troubled youth. Films like this, including *The Wild One* (1953) and *Blackboard Jungle* (1955), communicated the central dilemma in America's perception of its young people: were juvenile delinquents simply disruptive for no good reason or did society have to take some responsibility for the discontentment of teenagers who rejected the conformity of the era?

Catcher is not, then, the only text to resist the doctrines of its time and express 'the sense of alienation experienced by sensitive individuals in the midst of an oppressive mass culture'.[44] Arthur Miller's play *Death of a Salesman* (1949) shows the decline of Willy Loman, the salesman of the title, who commits suicide when he realises that he will never achieve the success promised by the American Dream (the belief that hard work will be rewarded by prosperity): like many victims of the 'rat race', he has spent his life working for a company that leaves him with nothing. While the best-selling novels of 1951, the year that *Catcher* was published, were concerned with the recent war – *From Here to Eternity* by James Jones, *The Caine Mutiny* by Herman Wouk and *The Cruel Sea* by Nicholas Monsarrat – the 1950s saw a growth in counter-cultural literature that *Catcher*

---

44 Tindall and Shi, *America: A Narrative History*, p. 1348.

seems to anticipate. Not least of these is Ralph Ellison's scathing assessment of the situation of African Americans, *Invisible Man* (1952), in which an unnamed narrator tells the story of his life's journey through a range of cruel and oppressive experiences in a country that will not acknowledge his rights because of his race. Later in the 1950s the 'Beat Generation' – principally the novelists Jack Kerouac (who began his key text, *On the Road*, in 1951), William Burroughs (*Junky*, 1953) and the poet Allen Ginsberg (*Howl*, 1956) – celebrated in experimental writing taboo experiences with drugs and sex.[45] The activities of HUAC (the government committee that aimed to expose and punish Communist sympathisers) made film-makers extremely cautious about the content of their films. The conventional escapism offered by musicals and romances remained popular; more subversive were science-fiction films that, while seeming to be entirely distant from everyday American life, were able to comment on it. *The Day the Earth Stood Still* and *The Thing* (both 1951), *It Came from Outer Space* (1953) and *Invasion of the Body Snatchers* (1956) are key examples of films that critique conformity and fear of the 'Other' through fantasies of alien invasion.

Non-conformity, then, was not entirely contained in the 1950s and although *I Love Lucy* and *Leave it to Beaver* – the classic television programmes of stable family life in this period – may have been far more famous to the average American, the rising counter-culture had a powerful and enduring impact. Innovations in the arts like be-bop jazz, abstract painting and innovative writing in all genres, along with film stars like James Dean and Marlon Brando, the rise of rock 'n' roll and even existentialist philosophy all contributed to destabilising the inflexible social fabric of the 1950s. Book sales rose, aided by the boom in cheap paperback editions that made all kinds of reading material – novels, social studies, 'pulp' fiction – widely available. *Catcher* itself benefited from this change in book production; had it only been available in hard covers, it might never have reached the huge student audience that read it avidly from the mid-1950s onwards. Although in many ways a product of the 1940s, *Catcher*'s increasing popularity in the 1950s shows how effectively it pinpointed issues that were central to post-war America.

Catcher and censorship

Given the social climate of the period in which *Catcher* appeared, it would be reasonable to expect the novel to meet with some hostility. The opinions of the early reviewers and the later literary critics will be discussed in Critical history (**pp. 35–66**), but there is another way in which *Catcher* has been understood: as a corrupting influence on young people. *Catcher* is 'both beloved *and* banned'.[46] Although it is taught in high schools and universities all over the world and is often voted a favourite novel in polls, it has been controversial in many American states. The first official complaint against the novel was made in 1955 and these have continued steadily to the present. In one well-documented and fairly typical

45 Ann Charters (ed.), *The Penguin Book of the Beats*, London: Penguin, 1992, p. 75.
46 Stephen J. Whitfield, 'Cherished and Cursed: Toward a Social History of *The Catcher in the Rye*', *New England Quarterly* 70, 1997, p. 574.

case of 1962, controversy raged in a California school about the assignment of *Catcher* (along with work by Arthur Miller and John Steinbeck) to eleventh-grade students. The novel, said one complainant, 'takes the Lord's name in vain 295 times and uses blatant blasphemy 587 times' and was the work of an author 'seemingly obsessed with the abnormal and debauchery'.[47] In 2004, to cite another representative example, school students in Maine asserted their right to read *Catcher* following an attempt to ban it on the grounds of its content and language.[48] Efforts to ban *Catcher* have revealed misunderstandings (J. D. Salinger has been confused with Pierre Salinger, who was John F. Kennedy's press secretary), have tapped into political anxieties (the novel has been accused of being Communist on the basis that its values are subversive) and exposed inconsistent attitudes, such as those of the parent whose complaint about the expletives in the novel included the question: 'How the hell did this teacher get this book?'[49] However varied the complaints, it is worthwhile considering what it is about *Catcher* that causes controversy and hostility, especially since teachers have been known to lose their jobs as a penalty for assigning the novel.

Catcher is not the only novel to face prohibition in the USA, and it is in good company: amongst others, Mark Twain's *The Adventures of Huckleberry Finn* (1885) has been banned for racial stereotyping and Toni Morrison's *The Bluest Eye* (1970) has been banned for its representation of poor 'family values'. Perhaps it is not really so difficult to understand why parents (and it is almost always parents who complain about the novel being assigned to tenth- or eleventh-grade school students) consider it inappropriate for their teenage children. After all, Holden Caulfield fails his exams catastrophically, leaves school but instead of going home spends three days wandering around Manhattan, drinks, smokes and swears, hires a prostitute and seems to end up in a psychiatric facility. If Holden is an appealing, sympathetic hero to many readers, is there a risk that his actions might be seen as acceptable? The fact that Mark Chapman, who murdered John Lennon in 1980, and John Hinckley, who attempted to assassinate President Ronald Reagan in 1981, were both associated with the novel (Chapman read aloud from it at his trial, while a copy was found in Hinckley's possession) has only served to intensify the controversy around *Catcher*. For some observers, the novel's association with criminals suggests that it has the power to shape the actions of disaffected outsiders and so teenagers should be shielded from its malign influence.

Yet *Catcher* was not intended for a teenaged audience. The concept that Holden is a poor role model for young people only arises when people of Holden's age are encouraged to read the novel, which has never been banned for an adult audience. Salinger consistently writes about children and adolescents, but not for them. Problems have arisen because the novel has become a text that is recommended to adolescents, perhaps on the assumption that it will help them to

47 Marvin Laser and Norman Fruman, 'Not Suitable for Temple City' in Marvin Laser and Norman Fruman, (eds), *Studies in J. D. Salinger: Reviews, Essays, and Critiques of The Catcher in the Rye and Other Fiction*, New York: Odyssey Press, 1963, p. 127.
48 Adam D. Krauss, 'Noble High Students Anxious to Read *The Catcher in the Rye*', 7 December 2004, <http://www.abffe.com/bbw-catcherintherye.htm>.
49 Whitfield, 'Cherished and Cursed', p. 576.

better understand their situation and, to some readers, *Catcher* remains the definitive novel of teenage experience. In the last part of this chapter, the text will be discussed in detail with the aim of pinpointing what is distinctive about it, exploring its language, structure, key moments and central themes; in the process, it may be possible to decide whether or not Holden Caulfield is really the archetypal adolescent he is often taken to be.

The Catcher in the Rye: detailed discussion

The Catcher in the Rye is a circular novel: it begins and ends in the same place at almost the same time. Arranged into twenty-six chapters, the novel could be understood to fall into four main sections, based on Holden's location and the day: at Pencey Prep (Saturday afternoon and evening, Chapters 1–7); at the Edmont Hotel (Saturday night, Chapters 8–14); public places in Manhattan (Sunday daytime and evening, Chapters 15–20); apartments in Manhattan (Sunday night to Monday morning, Chapters 21–24). Chapter 25, set during the day on Monday, when Holden meets up with Phoebe and he watches her on the carrousel in the rain, is the most fragmented chapter in the novel, building up to its key moment with a complex sequence of events in a range of locations. Chapter 26 is set a few thousand miles away from, and several months later than, the pre-Christmas Manhattan through which Holden has drifted in the preceding chapters.

The first paragraph of Chapter 1 establishes that Holden will tell 'you' the story of 'this madman stuff that happened to me around last Christmas just before I got pretty run-down and had to come out here and take it easy' (Ch. 1, p. 1); 'here' seems to be a facility near Hollywood where Holden is recovering from poor mental or physical health. The final, very short, chapter (Chapter 26) returns to this location as Holden concludes his narrative with 'That's all I'm going to tell about' (Ch. 26, p. 192). Within the frame of these first and last pages, the novel charts Holden's journey, physically from Pencey Prep to Manhattan and mentally to the point of revelation or breakdown, depending on interpretation, with Holden often stalling the forward progress of his narrative to draw on memories of other places and people that are provoked by his current situation. Throughout, Holden directs his story to 'you' and, although it is never quite clear who 'you' might be – a psychiatrist, a fellow patient? – the effect of this strategy is that the reader feels personally addressed by Holden and, as a result, intimately involved with him. This sense of connection between Holden and the reader is one of the key aspects of the novel's power.

Although the majority of the novel offers an extremely detailed account of Holden's experiences, both the opening and closing sections are paradoxically concerned with what Holden will not discuss. The text begins with his rejection of that 'David Copperfield kind of crap', meaning that he refuses to engage in conventional 'goddam autobiography' (Ch. 1, p. 1); it ends with allusions to what he 'could probably tell you', 'but I don't feel like it. I really don't' (Ch. 26, p. 192). The reference to Charles Dickens's novel *David Copperfield* (1849–50) is interesting, because *Copperfield* is a famed example of the *Bildungsroman* (or coming-of-age novel), a genre that *Catcher* is part of but simultaneously mocks by refusing to tell the story of its hero's journey to maturity, as convention dictates it should.

That David Copperfield is born with a 'caul' (a membrane) over his head playfully emphasises the link between Copper and Caul/field at the same time that Holden determines to tell a different kind of story by setting boundaries around what he is prepared to tell 'you' about his life.

Much of the opening paragraph is concerned with Holden's family although, interestingly, he focuses on the family members who feature least in the novel as a whole. His parents are '*nice* and all' but also 'touchy as hell' (Ch. 1, p. 1), and Holden seems conscious that his narrative must not reveal anything about them. This proves to be true, as the parents are never seen in the course of the novel: the closest contact between Holden and his mother comes when she talks to Phoebe and he hides in a cupboard to avoid her. Holden later describes his mother as 'nervous as hell. Half the time she's up all night smoking cigarettes' (Ch. 21, p. 143); he does not seem to see the similarity between this behaviour and his own. Holden's father is 'quite wealthy [. . .] a corporation lawyer' (Ch. 15, p. 97) who invests in Broadway shows and can afford to lose money on his investments; aside from this, Holden mentions his father very little and never in terms of emotion.

In the novel's opening paragraph, Holden also comments on his older brother D. B., a writer working in Hollywood. Holden claims to 'hate [. . .] the movies' (Ch. 1, p. 1) even though he obviously watches many films. It may be that what he hates most about the movies is that they, in the form of Hollywood, have turned D. B. into a 'prostitute' (Ch. 1, p. 1) who no longer writes 'terrific' short stories and cannot come home for Christmas (Ch. 21, pp. 147–8). The fact that D. B.'s story, 'The Secret Goldfish', sounds in its plot and title very much like a Salinger short story may offer a link to the author's own fears that money and fame corrupt artists. Later, Holden comments that he has gained his understanding that war is futile from D. B. who, again like Salinger, 'landed on D-Day and all' (Ch. 18, p. 126). Having identified these relatively minor characters and established the boundaries around what he will not tell 'you', Holden begins the story of his 'madman stuff' (Ch. 1, p. 1).

At Pencey

The first section of the novel (Chapters 1–7) is set during Holden's last day at Pencey Prep, focusing on his interactions with his teachers and his peers, principally Mr Spencer, Robert Ackley and Ward Stradlater. These episodes are interspersed with memories of Holden's sometime girlfriend, Jane Gallagher, and his deceased brother, Allie. Isolated on a hilltop watching the football game, Holden is 'trying to feel some kind of a good-by' (Ch. 1, p. 4) before he leaves the school: he is trying to come to terms with loss. This section establishes the themes of bereavement and leaving that characterise the novel as a whole. As he runs to Mr Spencer's house Holden has a feeling of 'sort of disappearing' (Ch. 1, p. 4) as he crosses the road, suggesting that he feels in danger of losing himself; this recurs much later in the novel when Holden crosses roads in Manhattan (Ch. 25, p. 178). At this early stage, Holden seems to attribute the experience to the kind of day it is – 'terrifically cold, and no sun out or anything' (Ch. 1, p. 4) – rather than to his troubled state of mind.

Mr Spencer is the first adult described in detail in the novel and Holden's discomfort with him is clear. Spencer's role as a teacher should make him a remote figure, but Holden's visit brings him across a boundary and places the two in an intimate situation; crossing such boundaries recurs in the novel. Spencer is ill and not fully dressed, but what disgusts Holden most is the teacher's age. Throughout the novel, the word 'old' is used in a range of ways but rarely to imply age: it can suggest the fake familiarity that Holden has learned from the hero of F. Scott Fitzgerald's novel *The Great Gatsby* (1925) ('old sport'); it can convey dull familiarity ('old Stradlater', 'old Sally') or communicate genuine intimacy and affection ('old Phoebe'). In relation to Spencer, however, Holden uses 'old' literally and almost excessively, indicating his disgust at seeing 'old guys in their pyjamas [. . .] Their bumpy old chests [. . .] Old guys' legs' (Ch. 2, p. 7). Holden's revulsion suggests that he fears the physical decline and vulnerability associated with ageing.

As well as their differences in age, Holden and Spencer are 'too much on opposite sides of the pole' (Ch. 2, p. 13): they disagree about whether 'life is a game', about whether it is fair to read aloud Holden's exam paper on Ancient Egypt, about whether Holden should feel concerned for his future. For Holden, Spencer's physical decline suggests not just ageing but death, a subject that fascinates and terrifies him. He feels 'sad as hell' (Ch. 2, p. 13) when he leaves Spencer because he thinks that he is, in a sense, leaving him to die. It is no coincidence that the recurring topic of the fate of the ducks in Central Park first arises when Spencer is lecturing him: Holden's mind drifts to this subject not because he is bored but because the ducks symbolise leaving and loss, subjects that are much on Holden's mind.

In this opening section of the novel, Holden's disdain for what he deems 'phony' is established. Patriarchal figures associated with school are phony: Haas, the headmaster at Holden's last school, because of his class prejudices (Ch. 2, p. 12); Ossenburger the undertaker because he implies that his financial success is related to his Christian observance (Ch. 3, p. 14). It is clear from comments Holden makes later that he admires strong people who do not overstate themselves, the nuns being an obvious example, especially in the contrast they offer to Ossenburger's pompous piety. Holden may be 'the most terrific liar you ever saw in your life' (Ch. 3, p. 14), but for him there is a substantial difference between lying and being phony: the former is simply telling an untruth for some reason, such as boredom or politeness, while the latter implies a person who has flawed values but who believes himself superior to others.

Holden's relationship with Ackley and Stradlater emphasises his in-between position because he identifies with both of them. Although he disparages Ackley for his poor personal hygiene and lack of social charm, he has sympathy for him. Stradlater, by contrast, has all the looks, charm and self-assurance that Ackley lacks, but Holden recognises Stradlater's deceptive quality as well as his appeal. Holden's perception that Stradlater has 'Year Book' (Ch. 4, p. 23) looks imply that he is photogenic, rather than genuinely handsome, and is a conformist whose persona matches the standards of the day. However, Holden enjoys his friendship with Stradlater: like a younger brother or son, Holden imitates movies to make Stradlater laugh while he is shaving (a strong signifier of adult masculinity), play fights with him (demonstrating Stradlater's superior strength) and is impressed by the older boy's sexual prowess, until he finds out that Jane Gallagher is to be Stradlater's date.

Holden's memories of Jane show that he sees her as a vulnerable figure, affectionate but sexually inexperienced, much like Holden himself. He is interested in details of her personality – such as the way she plays checkers (Ch. 4, p. 27) – that are irrelevant to Stradlater. Because their relationship is based as much on caring as desire, Jane is safe with Holden and he with her. Stradlater, however, even when dressed in Holden's jacket and groomed with Holden's 'Vitalis' (hair tonic), is very different from him. Stradlater is predatory and unscrupulous: the thought of him spending time with Jane makes Holden 'so nervous' that he 'nearly went crazy' (Ch. 4, p. 29). It is significant that, although Jane is nearby and even though Holden says three times that he will go to say hello to her, he never does; similarly, several times in later chapters, something always stops him from speaking to Jane on the telephone. These failures to reconnect are often explained away by the phrase 'I didn't feel like it', which allows Holden to avoid saying what he does feel. It may be that Holden is afraid to reconnect with Jane in case she has changed, perhaps by becoming sexually mature, a process that Holden fears because it implies the loss of innocence.

In the first paragraph of Chapter 6, words related to 'worry' appear six times, emphasising Holden's distraught state as he waits for Stradlater's return. In their ensuing argument and fight, the damage Stradlater inflicts on Holden is more than physical since he disdains two people central to Holden's life, Allie and Jane. By rejecting the essay that Holden has written for him about Allie's baseball glove, Stradlater implicitly denies Allie's importance; the reader recognises how inappropriate this is because Holden has described Allie in detail in the pages that immediately precede Stradlater's glib comments. Equally, the reader understands that Jane means much more to Holden than he is prepared to state explicitly and he dreads anything happening to her.

There are several references to hands in this section. Holden jokingly asks for Ackley's hand when he has his hat down over his eyes – 'Mother darling, give me your *hand*' (Ch. 3, p. 18) – positioning Ackley as Holden's mother and so mirroring Stradlater's role as a surrogate father. Allie's glove obviously evokes the hand, and Holden comments that he broke his fingers on the garage windows when Allie died and can no longer make a fist (Ch. 5, p. 34). Stradlater playfully 'socks' (Ch. 6, p. 37) Holden to try to appease him (and show that he is the more powerful of the two) after they disagree about the essay. These images culminate in violence: when Stradlater refuses to deny that he has had sex with Jane, Holden punches him. This implies a pattern: Holden responds with violence when he feels he has lost – literally or figuratively – someone he loves, be it Allie or Jane. In both cases, his mute action speaks his inexpressible pain.

Holden is in a desolate state after the fight: four times in Chapter 7 he comments on how 'lonesome' he feels, how he 'almost wished [he] was dead' and that he 'felt like jumping out the window' (Ch. 7, pp. 42–4). This last comment will echo across the novel, in images of falling and references to suicide. Holden decides to leave the school and check into a hotel: 'sort of crying' (Ch. 7, p. 46) as he goes, Holden is cutting himself adrift, rejecting both his peer group and the family home. Poignant as it is, the scene is undercut by a slapstick incident: after yelling a defiant '*Sleep tight, ya morons!*', Holden slips and almost breaks his 'crazy neck' (Ch. 7, p. 46) on peanut shells. Both funny and sad, like so much of the novel, this moment brings Holden's life at Pencey Prep to an end.

At the Edmont Hotel

The second section of the novel (Chapters 8–14) begins with Holden's train journey to Manhattan, during which he gets into conversation with an attractive older woman; ironically it transpires that her son is Ernest Morrow, 'the biggest bastard that ever went to Pencey' (Ch. 8, p. 48). Holden sees Mrs Morrow with a dual perspective: as a woman with 'quite a lot of sex appeal' and at the same time as a mother and therefore 'slightly insane' and not 'too sharp' (Ch. 8, pp. 49–50). By viewing her this way, his responses can remain at least partially non-sexual and therefore more manageable. His comments offer an insight into his views of his own mother – who appears in the text only as a voice – and his contradictory responses to women in general. For Holden, fondness for a woman is incompatible with sexual desire, since he believes sex to be taboo and sordid.

From Chapter 9 onwards, until the return to the California location in the final chapter, the novel is set in Manhattan, 'the supreme city in the Western world, or even the world as a whole' at the time.[50] *Catcher* contains many references to Manhattan landmarks (the Biltmore Hotel, Central Park, Bloomingdale's department store, Grand Central Station) that add to the novel's authenticity. Holden takes a cab to a hotel: the fact that he originally gives the driver his home address suggests that, unconsciously, he would like to go home. He asks the cabbie about the fate of the Central Park ducks in winter, although he believes that there is 'only one chance in a million' (Ch. 9, p. 54) that the driver will know, as if bird migration is not common knowledge. The driver thinks he is joking, so Holden's question goes unanswered and his anxieties about loss continue.

Once in his hotel room, Holden spends some time watching other guests, fascinated by the view from his window. 'That hotel was lousy with perverts', he comments, including a man doing 'something you wouldn't believe if I told you' (in fact, Holden does tell us: the man is cross-dressing) and a couple 'squirting water out of their mouths at each other' (Ch. 9, p. 55). Although Holden is excited by what he sees and claims, 'in my *mind*, I'm probably the biggest sex maniac you ever saw' (Ch. 9, p. 56), he is troubled by a confusing mixture of desire and anxiety. He says twice that he does not 'understand' sex and is obviously uncertain about the boundaries of sexual behaviour. His attempt to gain more sexual experience with Faith Cavendish goes no further than a stilted phone conversation in which both play the kind of phony roles that Holden despises.

Much of Chapter 10 is concerned with Phoebe, which suggests that the genuine connection Holden craves need not be sexual. 'You should see her. [. . .] You'd like her' (Ch. 10, p. 60) he comments, reinforcing the sense of intimate association between narrator and reader, between Holden and 'you'. Despite his usual negative assessment of the movies, Holden doesn't disparage Phoebe's fondness for the thriller *The 39 Steps* (1935) and, although Phoebe can be 'a little too affectionate sometimes' (Ch. 10, p. 61) – perhaps implying that she makes emotional demands

---

50 Jan Morris, *Manhattan '45*, Oxford: Oxford University Press, 1987, p. 7.

on him that he can't fulfil – she 'kills' Holden, a phrase he uses often to express how amusing or charming he finds someone. Here Holden says of Phoebe, 'she killed Allie, too. I mean he liked her, too' (Ch. 10, p. 61). Since the reader already understands that Holden's use of 'kill' is not literal, this explanation seems redundant, but the fact that he adds the extra information in relation to Allie may signify that he is never able to escape the sadness of his brother's death.

In need of distraction, Holden visits the 'Lavender Room', the hotel's night-club, where he meets three women (Bernice, Marty and Laverne) who hope to see a celebrity while they are visiting Manhattan. Holden's descriptions of them are unflattering and suggest that he sees himself as of a higher social class. Even so, he is 'about half in love with [Bernice] by the time we sat down' (Ch. 10, p. 65), continuing the theme of his confused responses to women, a mixture of desire and disdain for which he blames them as much as himself. Holden tells Marty that he has just seen the actor Gary Cooper, which could be read as a malicious lie that continues the novel's concern with phoniness (both that fame is phony and that Holden is himself being phony) or as a playful attempt to fulfil the girls' desire to brush with fame. Ultimately, Holden finds the girls depressing and, although he scorns the ideals of his own social class, he is patronising about the small-town values of Bernice and her friends, mocking their intellect and disparaging their pleasure in what he considers superficial.

The next chapter is dominated by thoughts of Jane, who represents the anti-thesis of the women Holden has just met. The intimacy he shares with Jane is not sexual and his realisation that 'You don't always have to get too sexy to get to know a girl' (Ch. 11, p. 69) suggests his emotional maturity. Holden's description of Jane suggests an appreciation for her that is more than physical and the terms he uses suggest that she provokes in him the deep affection he reserves for Phoebe and Allie: 'she knocked me out', she 'killed me' (Ch. 11, p. 70). Although he says that he likes to 'kid the pants off a girl' (Ch. 11, p. 70), which sounds sexual but actually expresses a desire for non-sexual play, the girls he likes most are the ones he does not want to kid, like Jane, for whom he does have sexual feelings. Despite their closeness, Holden and Jane have gone no further than kissing, perhaps because of Jane's difficult relationship with her stepfather. This chapter estab-lishes that, although aspects of Jane's life and personality remain obscure to him, Holden is not lying when he says he 'know[s] old Jane like a book' (Ch. 11, p. 69).

Depressed by his memories and the hotel, Holden decides to go a nightclub called Ernie's. In the cab, Holden once again seeks information about the ducks in Central Park; Horwitz the cabbie tells him that 'it's tougher for the *fish*' who have to take in nutrition through their 'pores' when frozen in the ice (Ch. 12, p. 75). Horwitz maintains that 'If you was a fish, Mother Nature'd take care of *you*, wouldn't she? Right?' (Ch. 12, p. 76), but Holden does not have the same cer-tainty: in his experience, some living things (like Allie) are simply allowed to die. Equally, some questions (about the ducks, about death) remain unanswered. As with the previous cabbie, Holden invites Horwitz for a drink, signifying his longing for company and connection, and once again his offer is refused.

Holden believes that Ernie, the nightclub pianist, plays for the audience rather than for the love of playing, which makes him phony: if Holden were a pianist, he says, he would 'play it in the goddam closet' (Ch. 12, p. 77) because the desire to please the audience corrupts the artist. It is difficult here not to think of Salinger, with his deep mistrust of publishers and his rejection of his readers. Conscious of being on his own, Holden only notices couples, including a 'Joe Yale-looking guy' (implying both the status and conformity associated with Yale University) with a 'terrific-looking girl' (Ch. 12, p. 78). They represent much of what Holden finds tawdry in sexual relationships: the young man, the epitome of respectability and privilege – a Stradlater figure – is telling his date about a suicide while 'giving her a feel under the table' (Ch. 12, p. 78), about which she is protesting. The boundaries of acceptable behaviour are being crossed again and the recurring subject of suicide arises: sex and death mix in this unpleasant scene.

'Then, all of a sudden, I got in this big mess' (Ch. 13, p. 82) is how Holden begins his description of one of the most significant and distressing sequences in the novel. Back at the hotel, 'against my principles and all' (Ch. 13, p. 82), Holden agrees to have a prostitute sent to his room. It is not difficult to understand why he gets into this situation: he is lonely, he is keen to gain sexual experience, and he is adrift in a situation in which conventional rules and boundaries have broken down. In another slapstick moment, Holden falls over his suitcase on his way to let the prostitute into his room, establishing the mix of dark comedy and pathos that will characterise the scene. Keen to 'get it over with' (Ch. 13, p. 84), Holden finds that he feels more depressed than aroused by his encounter with the inappropriately named Sunny. Her name is similar to Salinger's childhood nickname, suggesting perhaps that Salinger/Sonny, like D. B., is a prostitute in his writing, selling his art to anyone. This interpretation may be supported by the fact that Sunny tells Holden that she comes from 'Hollywood' (Ch. 13, p. 86), a further link to D. B. The more that Holden thinks of Sunny as an ordinary girl who should not have to sell her body, the less able he is to have sex with her and eventually he asks her if she minds if they do not 'do it' (Ch. 13, p. 87). Holden has empathy for Sunny, as he had for Jane: it is not that he lacks desire, but that he lacks the capacity to fulfil his own desires regardless of the cost to another. This response suggests that Holden is in some ways a mature person with moral values that shape his behaviour.

Shaken by his encounter with Sunny, Holden talks aloud to Allie, as he does 'sometimes when I get very depressed' (Ch. 14, p. 89), an act that will recur as Holden's situation becomes increasingly desperate. Despite being 'sort of an atheist' (Ch. 14, p. 89), Holden likes Jesus and feels the need to pray; in a sense talking to Allie 'sort of out loud' (Ch. 14, p. 89) is similar to praying. Holden's comments on Jesus and his disciples focus on Holden's belief that 'All they did was keep letting Him down' (Ch. 14, p. 89), which is both an interpretation of the Bible (in a novel that is interested in issues of truth and trust) and an image of an isolated individual, betrayed by those he should have been able to rely upon. Although it would be an overstatement to see Holden as a Christ figure, it is possible that his comments are shaped by his own sense of isolation; they also offer a pre-echo of the story of James Castle, the boy (with, like Christ, the initials J. C.) who committed suicide rather than acquiesce to a mob. Further, Allie is linked to both Castle and Christ, since he is figured as saint-like and was not saved from death by those whom he trusted.

Holden tries hard to stand his ground during his argument with Maurice, the intimidating 'bell-boy' (pimp) who demands extra cash from Holden for sex that he did not actually have. Unmoved by Holden's tears, Maurice justifies his rough treatment of Holden on the basis that Holden had agreed to pay Sunny ten dollars. However, the earlier conversation with Maurice (Ch. 13, p. 82) established that the agreement was for five dollars, which heightens the reader's empathy with Holden's sense of injustice. Maurice uses the difference in social class between them as a weapon, threatening to tell Holden's parents, and it is an insight into Holden's values that he is prepared to resist Maurice despite this vulnerability. Once Sunny and Maurice have left with his money, Holden feels as though he is 'drowning' (Ch. 14, p. 93), literally because he has been punched in the stomach and metaphorically because he is out of his depth.

Holden tries to shield himself from the reality of what has happened to him by acting out the role of a wounded hero from a movie, the sort of man who can be shot and yet still be able to take revenge on his attacker and call his girlfriend over to bandage him, smoking a casual cigarette as he does. Actors, of course, do not really get hurt – which is why they can so effortlessly portray unrealistic models of masculinity – and so Holden's imagination temporarily protects him from genuine emotional and physical pain. However, when the power of the fantasy wears off, Holden feels like 'committing suicide [. . .] jumping out the window' (Ch. 14, p. 94), echoing his earlier comments at Pencey and evoking James Castle once more. His claim that he only resists suicide because he could not bear to be seen by onlookers suggests that Holden is ashamed of his vulnerability – perhaps perceiving emotion as unmasculine – and does not wish it to be exposed.

Out in the city

As the third section (Chapters 15–20) begins, Holden once again considers phoning Jane and, as always, find that he is not 'in the mood' (Ch. 15, p. 95). Instead, he calls Sally Hayes, a girlfriend that he desires physically but obviously does not like very much, and arranges to take her to the theatre later that day. Over breakfast, he gets into conversation with two nuns. This is a good example of the ways in which Salinger has structured the narrative to accommodate the past within the present. Holden can share his thoughts about the nuns, who are a part of the unfolding sequence of events that he is describing and, within the same episode, offer an anecdote from his past. The nuns have 'inexpensive-looking suitcases' (Ch. 15, p. 97) which provokes Holden to recall a boy he roomed with at school, Dick Slagle. Dick obviously both resented and envied Holden's expensive suitcases and the wealth and privilege they represented; this social division ruined a potential friendship in a way that Holden finds sad but inevitable. This narrative strategy – using a detail about a character or place as a springboard into a completely different time and location – is very typical of Salinger's work and is used repeatedly throughout the novel, allowing him to offer greater insights into Holden's values and to subtly address issues that are more serious than the surface may suggest. So, in this example, Holden's digression allows us to see that he is not simply judgemental about those less fortunate than himself, but is uncomfortably aware of the tension created by inequalities in wealth and status.

Holden feels guilty about the nuns because he is aware that they have chosen to live without the privileges he casually enjoys. However, the scene with them is also concerned with issues related to sex and gender: they are women who have chosen to live without sexual relationships with men in a society that is particularly focused on marriage, believing that a woman's 'natural' place is in the home raising children. For these reasons, the nuns are desexualised outsider figures, very different from the women Holden knows. He finds it easy to talk to them, partly because he often empathises with outsider figures and partly because there is no pressure on him to interact with them on a sexual level. Holden's comments about Mercutio in Shakespeare's *Romeo and Juliet* are also revealing, as they seem to show how many of his responses are founded on his anxieties about death and his anger about unfairness. When he says of Mercutio, 'it drives me crazy if somebody gets killed – especially somebody very smart and entertaining and all – and it's somebody else's fault' (Ch. 15, p. 100), he is surely speaking about Allie. However, Holden is dealing here with issues of blame, too, and it may be difficult for him to accept that his brother's death was not anybody's fault. James Castle, by contrast, was driven to his death by others, and it is possible here that Holden's sense of injustice and grief, epitomised by Mercutio's fate, combines to account for both Allie and James.

Killing time before his date, Holden decides to buy Phoebe a record, 'Little Shirley Beans'. The singer performs the song 'very Dixieland and whorehouse', suggesting sexual innuendo, and the implication is that this is because she is black; a white singer would just be 'cute' (Ch. 16, p. 104). This suggests that there are ideas that Holden has absorbed from the prejudices of his moment that he does not reconsider, especially in relation to a subject like sex that he already finds confusing, or racial difference which, as a member of the white elite, he is not exposed to. On his way to buy the record, he sees a child walking in the road at the edge of the curb, singing 'if a body catch a body coming through the rye', unnoticed by his parents (Ch. 16, p. 104). Being neither fully in the road nor on the sidewalk, the boy symbolises Holden's own situation, caught between childhood and adulthood. The boy's parents do not seem to be paying him any attention; like Holden he is a lonely figure, vulnerable to the dangers of the city.

Shortly after this, Holden has encounters with other children: in Central Park he meets a girl Phoebe's age and two boys playing on a see-saw. In both cases he tries to prolong his contact with them, but – like the boy singing in the street – these children are self-contained and do not want his company, suggesting that there is a gulf between them that is less obvious to Holden than it is to the children. Between these two encounters, Holden decides to visit the Museum of Natural History, as he often did as a child. He is comforted to think that the exhibits he remembers are all as they were, including the Indians, the Eskimo and the migrating birds; this last suggests that whatever is fuelling his anxieties about the ducks in Central Park, it is not ignorance of migration. While he enjoys the feeling of familiarity offered by the exhibits, he finds that 'the best thing [. . .] in that museum was that everything always stayed right where it was. Nobody'd move' (Ch. 16, p. 109). In a life that is changing unbearably quickly, Holden finds reassurance in the stability and sameness that the exhibits offer. However, he realises that, even in the museum, there is change, because the visitors are a little different every time they visit; the children grow up, as he has done. So change is, after all, inevitable, even in the museum, however much Holden wishes that 'certain things they should stay the way they are' (Ch. 16, p. 110). Holden realises that he cannot bear to enter the museum; this is an interesting narrative device because the description is so vivid that it is easy to forget that Holden is only remembering the museum, not walking around it. Perhaps it has, in fact, changed; that may be why he will not venture inside.

Seeing Sally, Holden says: 'I felt like I was in love with her and wanted to marry her. [. . .] I told her I loved her and all. It was a lie, of course, but [. . .] I *meant* it when I said it' (Ch. 17, pp. 112–13). In sense, Holden cannot have been lying if he was sincere at the time; perhaps the lie comes from the fact that he is not able to perceive clearly what he feels and wants. However, he seems clear about what he dislikes: Holden considers the Lunts (the actors Alfred Lunt and Lynn Fontanne, a celebrated theatrical couple of the era) to be, like Ernie the pianist, 'too good' (Ch. 17, p. 113) and inclined to show off. His complaints to Sally continue and range widely, including the 'phony' they meet in the interval, school ('full of phonies'), cars ('I'd rather have a goddam horse') and his own state of mind ('I'm in *lousy* shape') (Ch. 17, pp. 114–18).

Some of these complaints are comic, some poignant; they express the instability and negativity of Holden's perceptions and also reveal him to be, potentially, an unreliable narrator. If a text has an omniscient narrator, it is possible to know what various characters are thinking and so gain a variety of perspectives. By contrast, when a narrative is written in the first person, the reader is totally reliant on the narrator for an understanding of what is happening in the text. If a first-person narrator is unreliable, the reader cannot be certain about what is taking place. As Holden tells Sally of his dissatisfactions, she asks him twice to speak more quietly ('Don't shout, please'; 'Stop screaming at me, please') and on both occasions Holden refutes that he is raising his voice ('I wasn't even shouting'; 'I wasn't even screaming at her') (Ch. 17, pp. 117–19). This contradiction leaves the reader with two possibilities: one is that Sally is self-conscious about Holden's behaviour and is worried that he will be overheard; the other is that Holden is, in fact, out of control and shouting, so distressed that he cannot see the truth about his own behaviour. The former explanation leaves us safely on Holden's side; the latter has much more troubling implications. It is typical of Salinger to leave the reader in a state of uncertainty; this strategy may allow us to empathise with Holden's uncertainties about what is genuine and what is 'phony'.

By the end of the conversation, Sally is in tears, having refused to run away with Holden who responds by telling her that she gives him 'a royal pain in the ass' (Ch. 17, p. 120). Holden's perception that escaping now is essential seems based on his conviction that once adulthood is attained, with all its attendant responsi-bilities and rituals – 'working in some office, making a lot of dough' (Ch. 17, pp. 119–20) – the later escape (or, for her, vacation) that Sally proposes will be impossible. Looking back, Holden acknowledges that he did not really want to run off with Sally but, as when he says that he loves her, he '*meant* it' (Ch. 17, p. 121) at the time. This confirms the inconsistency of Holden's perceptions: although seeking love and reassurance, he is so distraught that he no longer knows what exactly he believes and lashes out at people who cannot or will not fulfil his needs.

Unable to contact Jane, Holden goes to Radio City Music Hall (Manhattan's most famous concert hall/cinema) to pass the time. In contrast to Ernie and the Lunts, Holden has great affection for the man playing the kettle drums in the orchestra, which may derive from the fact that Allie liked him. Much like the exhibits Holden describes in the museum, the musician has been the same since Holden's childhood and so part of his appeal is his static quality; indeed, he literally hardly ever moves because he plays the drums infrequently during the show, emphasising his similarity to the museum pieces. Holden describes the film he watches in great detail: it is 'so putrid I couldn't take my eyes off it' (Ch. 18, p. 124). Its plot is similar to that of *Random Harvest* (1942) in which a veteran of the First World War loses his memory and begins a new life. To Holden it is as phony as the woman in the audience who is too busy weeping over the film to attend to the needs of her young son: her sentimentality conceals a lack of genuine kindness. The film's content can be linked to the more recent world war, which provokes some strong comments from Holden. D. B. (who has seen active service) told his brother that the army is 'full of bastards' (Ch. 18, p. 126), and Holden himself has no faith in the morality of war, claiming that he would rather be shot than fight for his country and that he will 'sit right the hell on top of [the atomic bomb]' (Ch. 18, p. 127) if there is ever another war. In post-war America, still celebrating the victory of 1945, these are radical views, more fitting to the Vietnam generation than the conservative 1950s.

Carl Luce, who Holden meets for a drink after his argument with Sally, is – as discussed earlier (see Text and contexts, **p. 11**) – an interesting figure whose detailed knowledge of the sexual preferences of film stars positions him as McCarthyesque. Certainly, he has terrified Holden and his friends with the implication that even 'tough guy[s]' (Ch. 19, p. 129) could be 'flits' (homosexuals), thus exacerbating Holden's sexual anxieties. Holden's questions about sex reveal his immaturity and, indeed, Luce asks him more than once when he is going to 'grow up' (Ch. 19, pp. 130–1); perhaps Holden is reverting to the role he played with Luce when they were at school together. Holden obviously admires Luce: although he concedes at the end of their meeting that Luce (like Sally) is 'strictly a pain in the ass' (Ch. 19, p. 134), he is impressed by Luce's 'vocabulary', his interest in 'Eastern philosophy' and his apparent wisdom. During their conversation he mirrors Luce's speech patterns: Luce uses the words 'relax' and 'listen' (Ch. 19, pp. 130–3) early in the discussion, after which Holden repeats the same words several times, suggesting that he sees Luce as a model to emulate.

Alone again and drunk, Holden returns to his fantasy of being shot in the stomach, playing out a movie role: 'I was con*ceal*ing the fact that I was a wounded sonuvabitch' (Ch. 20, p. 135). Holden is, of course, wounded (emotionally if not physically), and while he may be concealing that wound from himself and those he meets, it is becoming ever more clear to the reader. Leaving the bar, Holden is crying again, 'depressed and lonesome' (Ch. 20, p. 138). In Central Park, a recurrent location in the novel, Holden looks for the ducks at the lake but finds none, heightening his loneliness; he breaks Phoebe's record (like several people in the novel, it falls) but keeps the pieces. His fantasy in this sequence is not that he is wounded and surviving, but that he is ill and will die: imagining his funeral, he is at the same time imagining Allie's funeral, which he could not attend. His perception of his own death as principally a repeat of Allie's (even in terms of its impact on his mother) confirms how dominant a figure Allie is in Holden's life: he cannot understand himself without reference to his brother.

Going home

What could be called the final section of the novel begins with Holden's return to his family's apartment. The next three chapters (21–3) cover Holden's long talk with Phoebe, who is a typical Salinger character, much like the girls in 'For Esmé – With Love and Squalor' and 'A Perfect Day for Bananafish'. Honest and intelligent, capable of great insight because she is not adult, Phoebe is an engaging figure and Holden 'just felt good, for a change' (Ch. 21, p. 144) once reunited with her. Despite this more positive turn, references to death dominate these scenes with Phoebe. Apart from Holden's affectionate comments that Phoebe 'kills' him, Phoebe tells Holden that her role as Benedict Arnold (a general in the American Revolution, remembered for plotting treason) in the school play, 'starts out when I'm dying' (Ch. 21, pp. 146). Further, Phoebe has just seen a film in which a doctor commits euthanasia on a child (Ch. 21, pp. 146–7) and Holden is preoccupied by memories of Allie and James, both dead. Another reference to death comes when Phoebe works out that Holden has been expelled from school: her reaction is to exclaim several times, 'Daddy'll *kill* you' to which Holden responds three times, 'Nobody's gonna kill me', perhaps implying that he will kill himself (Ch. 21, p. 149).

Discussing his expulsion, Phoebe asks Holden 'Oh, why did you *do* it?' and he responds that he is 'sick of everybody asking me that' (Ch. 22, p. 151), which is interesting because only Mr Spencer seems to have asked him that question. Perhaps Holden is projecting onto others a question he is actually asking himself. All he can offer Phoebe by way of explanation is that Pencey was 'full of phonies. [. . .] I just didn't like anything that was *hap*pening at Pencey,' to which Phoebe responds, 'you don't like *any*thing that's happening' (Ch. 22, pp. 151–2). Salinger gives Holden and Phoebe almost the same words but indicates their different understanding with partially italicised words, a feature of his evocation of the rhythms of dialogue which is particularly pointed here because it suggests that a problem which Holden attributes to Pencey, Phoebe sees as a problem that derives from Holden. When Holden resists Phoebe's assertion, she challenges him to 'Name one thing' (Ch. 22, p. 153) that he likes, but his thoughts drift and he remembers James Castle. When he died, James was wearing Holden's sweater and so he is connected to Holden even though they were not friends; James has remained with Holden because of the injustice of his death. Although he has been thinking of James and of the nuns, Holden tells Phoebe that he likes her and Allie; she will not accept this answer on the grounds that 'Allie's *dead*' (Ch. 22, p. 154).

Changing tack, Phoebe asks Holden to name something he'd like to be; he rejects being a lawyer, since even an ethical lawyer might just be working for acclaim (like Ernie and the Lunts). Instead, Holden would like to be 'the catcher in the rye and all' (Ch. 22, p. 156), a fantasy role in which it is his responsibility to keep children safe as they play in a field, protecting them from physical harm and metaphorically keeping their childhood innocence safe by ensuring that they do not fall – become corrupted – as others have done (even Phoebe has taken a fall, having been pushed down stairs by a boy at school). Holden describes himself as being on the edge of 'some crazy cliff' (Ch. 22, p. 156) in this fantasy, suggesting his own vulnerability to falling as much as the children's; he sees himself as a protector, but there is no one in his vision who will save him.

Having called his old teacher Mr Antolini, Holden offers some information about him; especially significant is the fact that it was Antolini who picked up James's body. Perhaps Holden hopes that Antolini will offer him the same protection, though it is significant that Antolini did not 'catch' (save) James, but only attended to him after he had died. In the chapter at Antolini's apartment (Chapter 24), most of Holden's speech is contained in the opening pages; as the chapter goes on, Antolini talks more and Holden, exhausted, becomes almost silent. Holden's story about Richard Kinsella is significant, however, since it shows that Holden resents rules that restrict creativity, such as the prohibition on digressing in the Oral Expression class. Holden's repeated use of the phrase 'stick [or 'stuck'] to the point' (Ch. 24, p. 165) four times in as many sentences mimics the monotony of doggedly pursuing a single subject. Holden's admiration for rule-breakers, again – as with his anti-war stance – makes him seem more a part of the counter-culture than the conservative middle classes.

Continuing the novel's theme of falling children, Antolini tells Holden that he fears Holden is 'riding for some kind of a terrible, terrible fall' (Ch. 24, p. 168). Antolini seems to be suggesting that Holden will not fulfil his potential and will become a bored and bitter adult, hating other people for petty reasons. The terms Antolini employs are quite obscure; by the time that he is copying out what he perceives to be a key quotation from Wilhelm Stekel (an Austrian psychoanalyst), it is clear that his ideas are too complex for the moment and the audience. Antolini tells Holden that it is not enough to be brilliant and creative: one must be educated, too, and he believes that Holden will find his way if he returns to education. In a sense, Antolini is simply reiterating the points made by Holden's headmaster at Pencey, and Mr Spencer, and the teacher in oral expression: that rules are necessary and must be enforced, and that education is the route to success.

The final episode of the chapter is a sharp contrast to Antolini's speeches. The shift is signposted subtly: Antolini asks Holden about Sally and Jane ('How're all your women?'), comments on Holden's long legs, tells him that he will be in the kitchen (rather than in bed with his wife) and calls Holden 'handsome' (Ch. 24, pp. 171–2) before Holden falls asleep on the couch. Holden awakens to find Antolini touching his head. Antolini tells him that he is 'admiring –' something that remains undisclosed because Holden interrupts him, but Holden's comment that 'perverts' are 'always being perverty when *I'm* around' (Ch. 24, pp. 172–3) suggests that he could finish Antolini's sentence for him. Despite 'trying to act very goddam casual and cool and all' (Ch. 24, p. 173) Holden perceives Antolini's composure to be fake; he tells Holden twice that he is 'going to bed' (joining his wife) which could be read as a self-protective assertion of his heterosexuality. Whatever Antolini's intentions, which Salinger leaves ambiguous, Holden has been disappointed by an adult who seemed to promise sanctuary. Salinger may be reflecting the common prejudices of his era by including a homosexual character who is predatory; alternatively, he may be showing that Holden is inclined to leap to assumptions because of the society he lives in, especially if he has been subjected to unwanted sexual attention before and has been frightened by Luce's claims that 'flits' are everywhere.

The figure of the lecherous, closeted homosexual is a damaging cliché promoted by a bigoted and repressed society, but Salinger exposes this prejudice through Holden's reconsideration of Antolini in the following chapter (25). First, Holden attempts to desexualise the incident, which shows his capacity for forgiveness as well as his doubts about his own judgement. More importantly, Holden begins to think that 'even if [Antolini] was a flit he certainly'd been very nice to me', (Ch. 25, p. 175), which suggests that, while Antolini may have edged across a boundary, he is not a demon and his concern for Holden (and for Castle) is redemptive. There is no doubt, however, that Holden is confused and depressed by the incident and the magazine he reads in the station amplifies his fear of dying of cancer like Allie; Antolini has failed to 'catch' Holden and he is vulnerable and anxious once more.

It is in this state of despair that the final stage of Holden's journey begins. Wandering through Manhattan, Holden notices the signs of Christmas, a Christian celebration of family and faith. Holden, estranged from his fragmented family, finds no comfort in this; in fact, he is reaching crisis point. Crossing the street, Holden begins to fantasise that he will 'never get to the other side [. . .] I thought I'd just go down, down, down and nobody'd ever see me again' (Ch. 25, p. 178). Antolini's prediction that Holden is heading for a fall seems to be coming true, even if only in Holden's exhausted mind. As he has done before, Holden calls on Allie to help him cope: 'Allie, don't let me disappear. [. . .] when I'd reach the other side of the street without disappearing, I'd *thank* him. Then it would start all over again' (Ch. 25, p. 178). The sense that he is disappearing, especially when he tries to cross a literal or symbolic boundary (such as a road or a way of behaving) has been haunting Holden since he visited Mr Spencer. Disappearing, the loss of the self, inevitably evokes death, which is Holden's obsession. Now all that can save him from disappearing is faith in his dead brother: if no living person will catch Holden, perhaps Allie will.

To escape from this frightening sensation, Holden plans to run away, 'somewhere out West' (Ch. 25, p. 178), into the iconic frontier land of the USA where, perhaps, there will be freedom from the erasure of self that is overwhelming him. This retreat from society will involve not only a blue-collar job but pretending to be a deaf mute to avoid 'stupid useless conversations' (Ch. 25, p. 179). Holden's fantasy of leaving provokes a desire to say goodbye to Phoebe, as it did when he believed he was going to die of pneumonia and went home, so he goes to his sister's school. Like the museum, Phoebe's school is 'exactly the same as it was when [Holden] went there' (Ch. 25, p. 180), and he takes comfort from this static quality: the word 'same' is used six times in his description. Then he notices 'Fuck you' written on the school wall, an attack on innocence that 'drove [him] damn near crazy' (Ch. 25, p. 181) because he believes it will encourage children to discuss sex, projecting his fear of the subject onto a child. The violence of his reaction, which centres on beating the person who wrote the words 'till he was good and goddam dead and bloody' (Ch. 25, p. 181) expresses the extent of his alarm. Soon he sees another 'Fuck you' (Ch. 25, p. 182) that he cannot erase and he begins to realise the impossibility of protecting children from corruption: the impossibility of being the catcher in the rye. This gradual coming to terms proves to be a significant feature of the rest of the chapter.

Waiting for Phoebe, Holden goes to a place he feels sure has not changed: the museum. There he meets two boys who ask him to direct them to the 'mummies', which evokes preservation; once there, the boys take fright and leave Holden alone in the tomb, a place he finds peaceful until he sees yet another 'Fuck you' (Ch. 25, p. 183) on the wall. This suggests that there are no places untouched by corruption, which may be read as a comment on the post-war world, reeling from the impact of millions of deaths, or more specifically on the 'phoniness' and materialism of post-war America. Indeed, the moral decay is so extensive that Holden is certain that 'if I ever die [. . .] and I have a tombstone and all, it'll say "Holden Caulfield" [. . .] then right under that it'll say "Fuck you"' (Ch. 25, p. 183). In a novel so concerned with death, it is interesting to see Holden use the word 'if' in relation to his own, much-anticipated death; perhaps a tragic end is not inevitable after all.

Holden is still committed to his escape plan, despite passing out in the museum bathroom; he imagines allowing his family to visit him, as long as none of them did 'anything phony' (Ch. 25, p. 184). The implication of this is that Holden is less concerned with cutting himself off from people than with creating a place in which others must abide by his rules. As he thinks of this, Phoebe arrives, wearing Holden's hat and carrying his case: a smaller version of him, determined to join his adventure. Reacting harshly to her – perhaps because she exposes the impossibility of his plan – he tells her to shut up and resents her for being willing to miss her Christmas play, as if she is rejecting the innocence of childhood activities that he yearns to recapture. Phoebe mirrors Holden in various ways and, like him, she refuses to go back to school; her behaviour shows Holden how alike they are, but also that Phoebe is a child and that he is not anymore.

This recognition is vital to the final scene in the chapter, when Phoebe rides the carrousel and Holden watches her. Like the museum, the school and the kettle-drum player, the carrousel is a feature of Holden's past, still playing the same song that it used 'about fifty years ago when *I* was a little kid' (Ch. 25, p. 189), an exaggeration which suggests that his childhood now seems distant to him. Phoebe worries that she is 'too big' (Ch. 25, p. 189) for the carrousel; Holden assures her that she is not but, as he takes his seat with the adults, confirms that he is. This realisation of his own maturity and the necessity of allowing children to grow up culminates in his recognition that they have to be allowed to reach for the 'gold ring' on the carrousel: 'if they want to grab for the gold ring, you have to let them do it, and not say anything. If they fall off, they fall off, but it's bad if you say anything to them' (Ch. 25, p. 190). Children must be allowed to make their own mistakes; they cannot be shielded from every threat, imagined or real.

In the final paragraph, Holden sits in the rain, wearing his red hat, almost crying but 'so damn happy, if you want to know the truth' (Ch. 25, p. 191). Not sheltering with the parents or riding with the children, Holden seems to have come to terms with his in-between position. Intimate with the reader as he has been all along, he comments, 'I wish you could have been there' (Ch. 25, p. 191). There is a strong sense that much of Holden's fear has lifted: he cannot protect Phoebe from every possible hurt but he does not have to; he is neither adult nor child but that is not a disaster. Phoebe revolves on the carrousel, moving but not going away, changing slowly but not disappearing, and Holden can do the same. In this sense, the carrousel acts as a metaphor for the process of growing up. The realisation that change does not have to mean death, loss or corruption would seem to be the moment of epiphany that Holden has been searching for all along.

How the reader interprets what Holden is doing in California – the location established in the novel's first paragraph, to which the narrative returns in Chapter 26 – depends on how the preceding chapter has been understood. If he has indeed had a revelation at the carrousel, then perhaps the novel documents the full extent of his breakdown; in that case, he may just be in hospital to recover from a physical illness. By contrast, if the novel charts the progress of his breakdown to a moment of final collapse then he may be in California to heal mentally. At the end of his narrative, Holden refuses to discuss the future, just as he refused to discuss the past at the beginning of the novel. He denies that anyone knows 'what you're going to do till you *do* it' (Ch. 26, p. 192): although this evokes the random behaviour Holden exhibited throughout the novel, there is a sense at last that this level of uncertainty no longer frightens him. Whatever Holden may have gained from his experiences remains obscure to him: 'If you want to know the truth, I don't *know* what I think about it' (Ch. 26, p. 192). Holden, who hates anything phony, has to be honest and admit that the truth is not always apparent. *Catcher* closes with a poignant comment which suggests that Holden may not yet be convinced of the value of the intimate disclosure that constitutes his story: 'Don't ever tell anybody anything. If you do, you start missing everybody' (Ch. 26, p. 192). Perhaps surprisingly, after all Holden has been through, the implication is that his sense of loss has actually been intensified by the experience of telling 'you' about 'this madman stuff that happened to me' (Ch. 1, p. 1). This might mean that the healing process is not complete after all or, if considered in a more positive light, Holden may finally have come to realise the value of those who are still in his life as well as those he has lost.

2

Critical history

Hundreds of essays have been written about *The Catcher in the Rye* since it was published. This chapter, which surveys some of the most important and interesting criticism, is divided into four sections: the first considers the reviews that appeared in newspapers and magazines when *Catcher* was published; the second discusses the surge of academic criticism that began in the late 1950s and continued into the 1960s; the third chooses the most notable essays from a less active period in criticism of *Catcher*, the 1970s and 1980s; the last explores the new readings of the novel published in the 1990s and the 2000s, a period that saw a resurgence of interest in *Catcher*.

'Unbalanced as a rooster on a tightrope': reviews on publication

Catcher was chosen by the very influential Book-of-the-Month Club to be its summer choice for 1951. Perhaps unsurprisingly, Clifton Fadiman gave the novel a strong review in the Book-of-the-Month Club newsletter: 'That rare miracle of fiction has again come to pass: a human being has been created out of ink, paper and the imagination.'[1] Responses to the novel were generally positive, though a few critics disliked it intensely. Reviews tended to focus on issues of form, particularly Salinger's creation of a unique voice for Holden and on the social implications of the novel, perhaps inevitable given the increasing interest in adolescence in the post-war period (see Texts and contexts, **p. 16**). Discussion of events in the plot occurred less frequently and the focus was on Holden as a troubled figure with little said about the other characters.

Several reviewers, including those with positive comments to make, were uncomfortable with Salinger's use of expletives: 'ugly words [. . .] from the mouths of the very young and protected [are] peculiarly offensive', commented

---

1   Laser and Fruman, *Studies in J. D. Salinger*, p. 7.

Virgilia Peterson in the *Herald Tribune*.[2] For the anonymous reviewer in *Catholic World*, the novel was rendered 'monotonous and phony by the formidably excessive use of amateur swearing and coarse language'.[3] The *Times Literary Supplement* agreed that 'the endless stream of blasphemy and obscenity in which [Holden] thinks, credible as it is, palls after the first chapter'.[4] That issue of credibility was raised by several reviewers, often in praise. Harrison Smith in the *Saturday Review* asserted that the 'magic of this novel [depends] on the authenticity of the language [Holden] uses and the emotions and memories which overwhelm him'.[5] Harvey Breit in the *Atlantic Monthly* conceded that Holden is 'bright, terrible and possibly normal' and suggested that, however challenging Holden's thoughts and actions might be for some readers, he is not a fantasy but a recognisable figure.[6] The *Times Literary Supplement* was also prepared to believe that Holden was 'a very normal specimen of his age' and found him 'really very touching', but was obviously uncomfortable with an aspect of the novel that others praised, namely its commitment to Holden's point of view: 'One would like to hear more of what his parents and teachers have to say about him.'[7] By contrast, Virgilia Peterson contended that only Holden's peers would be able to judge the narrative's effectiveness: 'The question of authenticity is one to which no parent can really guess the reply.'[8]

T. Morris Longstreth, the reviewer for the *Christian Science Monitor*, presented the most negative of all reviews, finding nothing to praise and fearing the potentially negative influence of the novel. He perceived Holden to be 'alive, human, preposterous, profane and pathetic beyond belief. Fortunately, there cannot be many of him yet. But one fears that a book like this given wide circulation may multiply his kind.'[9] This anxiety could be read as confirmation of the authenticity of the novel: Holden's potential to influence others is perhaps a product of the accuracy with which he is portrayed. If influence is an issue – and it is one that has long troubled parents and school boards (see Texts and contexts, **pp. 17–19**) – then the novel's target audience must be considered. Longstreth was in no doubt that *Catcher* is 'not fit for children to read', but for Harold L. Roth of the *Library Journal* it was not intended for children anyway: Roth described it as an '*adult* book (very frank) and highly recommended'.[10]

Many reviewers affirmed Roth's judgement that the novel was not aimed at readers of Holden's age through analysis that focused on the ways in which *Catcher* used an adolescent perspective to critique adult society. *Booklist's* reviewer praised the novel for its 'sensitive insight into a currently important topic' – meaning adolescence – and Virgilia Peterson found in it proof that 'our youth today has no moorings'.[11] Others agreed with Nash K. Burger of the *New*

2 Laser and Fruman, *Studies in J. D. Salinger*, p. 9.
3 Joel Salzberg (ed.), *Critical Essays on Salinger's The Catcher in the Rye*, Boston, Mass.: G. K. Hall, 1990, p. 31.
4 Laser and Fruman, *Studies in J. D. Salinger*, p. 17.
5 Salzberg, *Critical Essays*, p. 29.
6 Harold Bloom (ed.), *Holden Caulfield*, Philadelphia, Pa.: Chelsea House, 1990, p. 6.
7 Laser and Fruman, *Studies in J. D. Salinger*, p. 17.
8 Laser and Fruman, *Studies in J. D. Salinger*, p. 9.
9 Bloom, *Holden Caulfield*, p. 6.
10 Laser and Fruman, *Studies in J. D. Salinger*, pp. 12, 7.
11 Laser and Fruman, *Studies in J. D. Salinger*, pp. 7, 8.

York Times, who believed that Holden's 'failings are not of his own making but of a world that is out of joint', and with Harvey Breit, who was convinced that 'for all its surface guilelessness, [*Catcher*] is a critique of the contemporary, grown-up world'.[12] Ernest Jones thought that the novel was easy to relate to, which he considered a serious weakness:

> As [the novel] proceeds on its insights, which are not really insights since they are so general, *The Catcher in the Rye* becomes more and more a case history of all of us. Radically this writing depends on the reader's recollection of merely similar difficulties; the unique crisis and the unique anguish are not recreated.[13]

For Jones, the sense that the novel 'merely' required him to acknowledge that he had sometimes felt as Holden did mean that the rewards for reading were limited: 'though always lively in its parts, the book as a whole is predictable and boring'.[14]

Some reviewers praised the novel for its humour and identified Holden's voice as the key source. S. N. Behrman commented in the *New Yorker*: 'The literalness and innocence of Holden's point of view in the face of the tremendously complicated and often depraved facts of life make for the humor of this novel [. . .] Holden's contacts with the outside world are generally extremely funny.'[15] R. D. Charques, writing in *The Spectator*, offered cautious praise: 'Though a little showy in effect, the style of the book is quite a performance. [. . .] Intelligent, humorous, acute and sympathetic in observation.'[16] William Poster considered the evocation of Holden's voice to be the novel's main strength, acclaiming Salinger's 'perfectionist handling of contemporary idiom'.[17] Harvey Breit affirmed the quality of Salinger's wit, but was not convinced that humour was the most effective strategy: 'Whatever is serious and implicit in the novel is overwhelmed by the more powerful comic element. What remains is a brilliant *tour de force*, one that has sufficient power and cleverness to make the reader chuckle and – rare indeed – even laugh aloud.'[18] So what Behrman admired as 'a dark whirlpool churning fiercely below the unflagging hilarity of the surface activities', suggesting that the novel's seriousness remained evident despite its enjoyable humour, was for Breit more problematic: the novel's humour is so accomplished that it distracts the reader from important issues that the text might have raised.[19] Perhaps inevitably, one reviewer could not resist the temptation to try writing in 'Holden-ese': 'This Salinger, he's a short story guy. And he knows how to write about kids,' wrote James Stern in the *New York Times*, 'This book, though, it's too long. Gets kind of monotonous. And he should've cut out a lot about those jerks and all at that crumby school.'[20]

T. Morris Longstreth may have considered Holden to be 'as unbalanced as

12 Laser and Fruman, *Studies in J. D. Salinger*, pp. 10, 14.
13 Laser and Fruman, *Studies in J. D. Salinger*, pp. 15–16.
14 Laser and Fruman, *Studies in J. D. Salinger*, p. 16.
15 Laser and Fruman, *Studies in J. D. Salinger*, p. 13.
16 Laser and Fruman, *Studies in J. D. Salinger*, pp. 16–17.
17 Salzberg, *Critical Essays*, p. 26.
18 Laser and Fruman, *Studies in J. D. Salinger*, p. 14.
19 Laser and Fruman, *Studies in J. D. Salinger*, p. 13.
20 Laser and Fruman, *Studies in J. D. Salinger*, p. 9.

a rooster on a tightrope' and his narrative 'quick-moving, absurd and wholly repellent in its mingled vulgarity, naiveté, and sly perversion', but few other reviewers condemned it completely.[21] Virgilia Peterson also expressed some doubts but concluded that the novel had both strengths and weaknesses: 'At best [it] has a truly moving impact and at worst is casually obscene.'[22] In general, most reviewers – despite anxieties about the novel's language or its implications – found much to enjoy and admire in its technique and protagonist, one commenting that it is 'an unusually brilliant first novel', another that it has a final scene that is 'as good as anything that Salinger has written, which means very good indeed'.[23] Harrison Smith's certainty that *Catcher* is 'a book to be read thoughtfully and more than once' would prove to be true for millions of readers in the half-century that has passed since he was asked to review the first novel by the promising young short-story writer, J. D. Salinger.[24]

Catcher received around 200 reviews when it was published, most of them very brief. Even those who admired it surely could not have predicted its future sales figures, let alone the prestigious place it would come to occupy in American culture. Initial sales, though impressive, did not indicate a future literary phenomenon, and Salinger's retreat from the public arena should have had a further negative impact on the novel's place in public consciousness. However, *Catcher* continued to sell steadily, with the appearance of a paperback edition in 1953 broadening its readership considerably, especially among younger people. University students played a significant role in spreading the word to their peers about the importance of the novel, and before long university lecturers became interested in the novel, including it on courses in contemporary fiction and writing academic analyses of it; this trend gained increasingly strong hold from the late 1950s and into the 1960s. As described in Texts and contexts (**pp. 1–34**) this was an era dominated in the USA by the growth in youth culture (to which *Catcher* spoke with great clarity and relevance), the 'Beat' writing movement (whose anti-establishment ethos is prefigured by Holden's disenchantment) and political activism that centred on anti-war protests and the civil liberties of a range of previously disenfranchised people. Holden Caulfield's narrative now seemed more significant than ever and Salinger's celebrity, far from fading, grew with every new group of readers who found in Holden a representation of their own feelings.

'One of the loneliest characters in fiction': the first wave of criticism (1950s and 1960s)

In 1958 critics Frederick L. Gwynn and Joseph L. Blotner noted in their study of J. D. Salinger that 'it is not inconceivable that some day Holden Caulfield may be as well known an American boy as Huck Finn'.[25] In part, this comment was

21 Bloom, *Holden Caulfield*, p. 5.
22 Laser and Fruman, *Studies in J. D. Salinger*, pp. 8–9.
23 Laser and Fruman, *Studies in J. D. Salinger*, pp. 10, 11.
24 Laser and Fruman, *Studies in J. D. Salinger*, p. 8.
25 Frederick L. Gwynn and Joseph L. Blotner, *The Fiction of J. D. Salinger*, Pittsburgh, Pa.: University of Pittsburgh Press, 1958, p. 29.

prompted by the success of *Catcher*, but it also recognises that Mark Twain's *The Adventures of Huckleberry Finn*, one of the best-loved novels in American literature, had become a common point of comparison for critics of *Catcher*. There are several reasons why these two novels were so often discussed in relation to each other – these will become clear in the discussion that follows – but the effect of the comparison was just as significant. By making connections between *Huckleberry Finn*, a canonical work of American fiction (that is, a work whose status as a 'classic' seems absolutely beyond question) and the expletive-heavy, disaffected, melancholy narrative of Holden Caulfield, critics were clearly asserting that *Catcher* was an important novel, deserving of close academic analysis. There is, obviously, a circular quality to this strategy: critical studies occur because the novel is important; because of the critical studies, the work is seen to be important. It is interesting that *Catcher*, a novel that was originally praised (and criticised) for its originality (or shock tactics), comes – initially at least – to be assessed by scholars as a text whose value lies in its close relationship with *Huckleberry Finn*, a much older and more conventional text.

In 1956, Arthur Heiserman and James E. Miller, Jr. published what is probably the first academic appraisal of *Catcher*. They asserted its importance as a part of two traditions: the American literary heritage exemplified by *Huckleberry Finn* and the European heritage of the quest narrative. The quest can be identified in mythological and medieval texts and is concerned with the journey of an individual to attain an object or goal. This narrative form is 'perhaps the most profound in western fiction. The [quest] is the central pattern of the epic.'[26] Reading *Catcher* in terms of 'epic' (a long, serious narrative of a hero's struggle to overcome many challenges) places it in elevated company: along with European antecedents stretching as far back as Homer's *Odyssey*, major literary figures of the twentieth century – James Joyce, William Faulkner – were part of that same tradition. Heiserman and Miller argued that quests come in two forms: in one, the protagonist leaves home in search of adventure (and personal growth); in the other, he is trying to find his way home. Unusually, Holden 'seems to be engaged in both sorts of quests at once; he needs to go home and he needs to leave it': because he find the society he lives in unbearably phony, he has to leave, but because he craves stability and love, he longs to stay.[27] Despite the sadness of this situation, Heiserman and Miller note the humour that characterises the novel; it is this aspect that most strongly evokes the voice of Huck Finn although, in addition, both boys are on a journey and both seek security in a corrupt world. Holden's first-person narrative is repetitive and digressive, but it offers – like that of Huck Finn – total access to the character: 'By the time we have finished *Catcher* we feel that we know Holden as thoroughly as any biography could reveal him.'[28] Like some of the novel's early reviews, Heiserman and Miller conclude that *Catcher* offers a critique of modern America by allowing the reader to see the impact of society on a person who refuses to compromise: 'It is not Holden who

26 Arthur Heiserman and James E. Miller, Jr., 'J. D. Salinger: Some Crazy Cliff', *Western Humanities Review* 10, 1956, p. 129.
27 Heiserman and Miller, 'J. D. Salinger: Some Crazy Cliff', p. 131.
28 Heiserman and Miller, 'J. D. Salinger: Some Crazy Cliff', p. 136.

should be examined for a sickness of the mind, but the world in which he has sojourned and found himself an alien.'[29]

Charles Kaplan must have been writing his essay on *Catcher* and *Huckleberry Finn* at the same time as Heiserman and Miller, because it was published in the same year. Less concerned with the European tradition, Kaplan focuses on connections between Holden and Huck and the ways in which both novels offer the reader an insight into societies that the narrators themselves often don't understand: 'Huck Finn and Holden Caulfield are true blood-brothers, speaking to us in terms that lift their wanderings from the level of the merely picaresque to that of a sensitive and insightful criticism of American life.'[30] Kaplan sees parallels between the two novels in terms of the first-person narrative technique, the colloquial language employed, the non-conformity of both protagonists, the journey both undertake and most of all the moral quality of the novels. This may be a surprise to those who seek to ban *Catcher* for its negative qualities, but Kaplan reads both Huck and Holden as figures of moral depth who are forced to reject the values of a society they see as corrupted. For Kaplan, the links between the two novels show not only *Catcher*'s place in an important literary tradition (thus asserting the validity of the novel) but also that both texts, although separated by more than sixty years, 'deal obliquely and poetically with a major theme in American life, past and present – the right of the nonconformist to assert his nonconformity'.[31] In Kaplan's estimation, then, Holden's rejection of his society, far from being evidence of his dysfunction, proves his moral worth and his value as an archetypal American hero.

Edgar Branch also considered *Catcher* to be 'a kind of *Huckleberry Finn* in modern dress' and, like Heiserman, Miller and Kaplan, saw in the novel both a critique of modern America and a moral protagonist.[32] Branch's focus, however, is on the ways in which the figure of Jim (the slave who becomes Huck's friend on their journey along the Mississippi) is paralleled in Salinger's text. One possibility is Mr Antolini, who is 'Holden's last adult refuge in his disintegrating world'; another is the recurring image – if not the actual presence – of Jane; a third is 'all little children, whom [Holden] would save from adult sexuality'.[33] Despite Holden's commitment to all of these figures, however, he remains 'desperately in need of love, [. . .] one of the loneliest characters in fiction'.[34] The implication of these early studies of *Catcher* is that Holden is a fictional character recognisable from an established literary tradition; that, despite its humour, it is a serious novel with important implications for post-war society; that Holden's moral stance against what he deems phony comes at the price of alienation when what he most desires is love and stability. Although Frederic I. Carpenter contended that *Catcher* and *Huckleberry Finn* do have their differences, not least that Huck is a 'typical American democrat' while Holden is a 'snob', he agreed that, fundamentally, Holden's 'New York and its problems are perhaps as central to modern

29 Heiserman and Miller, 'J. D. Salinger: Some Crazy Cliff', p. 137.
30 Charles Kaplan, 'Holden and Huck: The Odysseys of Youth', *College English* 18, 1956, pp. 76–7.
31 Kaplan, 'Holden and Huck', p. 80.
32 Edgar Branch, 'Mark Twain and J. D. Salinger: A Study in Literary Continuity', *American Quarterly* 9, 1957, p. 145.
33 Branch, 'Mark Twain and J. D. Salinger', pp. 144, 145.
34 Branch, 'Mark Twain and J. D. Salinger', p. 145.

America as Mark Twain's Mississippi River was to the pioneer nineteenth century'.[35] In some ways, Holden's problems are those of America itself: the nation's rise to power had been disorienting and now, like Holden, it must 'face [the] problems of growing up'.[36]

Whatever these essays tell us about the relationship between Holden and Huck and therefore *Catcher*'s place in the literary tradition, they also assert that Salinger's novel is one that demands and repays close critical attention. In so doing, these critics paved the way for the hundreds of essays that would follow. In the explosion of *Catcher* criticism during the 1950s and 1960s new pathways into the novel seem to be identified so often that the wealth of material is overwhelming. This section will identify and discuss some of the most interesting and useful approaches of the period.

By 1959, when he published his essay on language in *Catcher*, Donald P. Costello had become aware of the comparisons made with *Huckleberry Finn*. What Costello found interesting about this connection was not what it implied about the literary value of *Catcher* but the ways in which Holden's voice evoked Huck's. Costello also realised that many of the reviews of 1951 had been convinced that Salinger had recreated 'a true and authentic rendering of teenage colloquial speech', even if some reviewers had been reluctant to accept that obscenity was central to such speech.[37] Costello's essay aims to do more than the previous essays and reviews have achieved: he wants to analyse Holden's language, rather than just affirm its authenticity.

Costello suggests that the strength of the novel lies in the way that Salinger has utilised typical aspects of teenage speech yet still made Holden an individual: 'This difficult task Salinger achieved by giving Holden an extremely trite and typical teenage speech, overlaid with strong personal idiosyncrasies.'[38] Costello goes on to analyse in detail how this mixture of the typical and the idiosyncratic works in Holden's language. He identifies certain phrases ('and all', 'I really did', 'It really was', 'or something', 'or anything', 'if you want to know the truth') and notes that these phrases come to express Holden's character, not because they are in themselves especially interesting, but through their repetition. Other repetitious aspects of Holden's speech are interesting because their meaning is never stable: 'goddam', 'hell', 'ass', bastard', 'sonuvabitch', and other examples of the expletives for which the novel was condemned, are not necessarily as strong when Holden uses them as one might anticipate. This is partly because they don't have a stable meaning: the same word can mean its opposite in different contexts. For example, 'we had a helluva time' (Ch. 25, p. 177) means 'we had a good time' and the positive connotations lighten the impact of the expletive. Costello also notes that, despite Holden's 'bad' language, he has standards: although the phrase 'fuck you' appears in the novel, Holden never speaks it to another person in the novel, nor does he address the reader with expletives.

Examining Holden's choices of adverbs, adjectives and figures of speech, Costello is forced to agree with Holden's own assessment: he has a 'lousy

35 Frederic I. Carpenter, 'The Adolescent in American Fiction', *The English Journal* 46, 1957, p. 315.
36 Carpenter, 'The Adolescent in American Fiction', p. 316.
37 Donald P. Costello, 'The Language of *The Catcher in the Rye*', *American Speech*, 34, 1959, p. 172.
38 Costello, 'The Language of *The Catcher in the Rye*', p. 173.

vocabulary' (Ch. 2, p. 8). However, Costello notes that the effect of 'pil[ing] one trite adjective upon another [can produce] a strong power of invective', as in 'get your dirty stinking moron knees off my chest' (Ch. 6, p. 39).[39] Equally important to Holden's voice is the way that Salinger mixes quite advanced words in with the colloquialisms ('ostracized', 'exhibitionist', 'unscrupulous') and uses both formal terminology as well as slang phrases (Holden uses both 'take a leak' and 'relieve himself').[40] Sometimes the 'high' and 'low' speech forms appear together in the same phrase, as when Phoebe is 'ostracizing the hell out of' Holden (Ch. 22, p. 150). All of these strategies contribute to the comic effect of the novel.

Costello's lengthy analysis identifies a range of telling details about Holden's narrative, not least that the novel does, in fact, evoke spoken language rather than more formal writing. This is communicated in a number of ways, including direct repetition and fragmented comments: 'I sort of missed them. I mean I sort of missed them' (Ch. 24, p. 168). The novel also contains many grammatical errors that Holden, as a well-educated boy, might be expected to avoid: 'I used to play tennis with he and Mrs Antolini' (Ch. 24, p. 163), for example. These patterns and mistakes suggest, says Costello, that 'Salinger thinks of the book more in terms of spoken speech than written speech', because spoken language can be grammatically awkward in ways that would usually be ironed out in writing.[41] The characteristics of speech are also communicated through the use of italics for emphasis, sometimes for only part of a word, such as 'I haven't the *faint*est idea' (Ch. 19, p. 130). Costello concludes that the novel is as rewarding for a linguist as for a literary critic, but that the language of *Catcher* is 'only one part of an artistic achievement': a rather muted ending to a very detailed and useful essay that moves away from the *Huckleberry Finn* comparisons.[42]

Another key essay of *Catcher* criticism appeared in 1961: Carl Strauch's analysis of the structure of the novel. Strauch was aware of the use earlier critics had made of *Huckleberry Finn* but believed that all existing criticism had failed to recognise that:

> Salinger sharply accentuates the portrayal of Holden with a symbolic structure of language, motif, episode, and character; and when the complex patterns are discovered, the effect is to concentrate our scrutiny on a masterpiece that moves effortlessly on the colloquial surface and at the same time uncovers, with hypnotic compulsion, a psychological drama of unrelenting terror and final beauty.[43]

Strauch contends, then, that *Catcher* is far more complex than it has previously been understood to be. His long, demanding essay attempts to delineate that complexity and affirm the literary depth of Salinger's best-seller, trying to understand how it works in its own right, rather than only in relation to pre-existing literary traditions or earlier texts. Strauch's central argument is that Holden does

39 Costello, 'The Language of *The Catcher in the Rye*', p. 178.
40 Costello, 'The Language of *The Catcher in the Rye*', p. 179.
41 Costello, 'The Language of *The Catcher in the Rye*', p. 180.
42 Costello, 'The Language of *The Catcher in the Rye*', p. 181.
43 Carl F. Strauch, 'Kings in the Back Row: Meaning through Structure: A Reading of Salinger's *The Catcher in the Rye*', *Wisconsin Studies in Contemporary Literature*, 2, 1961, p. 6.

not need psychiatric help because he cures himself in the scene with Phoebe on the carrousel: the novel's pattern is of 'neurotic deterioration, symbolical death, spiritual awakening, and psychological self-cure'.[44] In the course of his essay, Strauch explains in detail how he sees this pattern working.

In this reading, Holden's visit to Central Park, followed by his trip home to see Phoebe are key to the text: 'Central Park represents Holden's [. . .] Dark Night of the Soul [. . .]; the paradise of his childhood is bleak, and the ducks that, in his fantasy, he has substituted for the human, have vanished. In effect, Holden is finished with childhood and is prepared for the burdens of maturity.'[45]

Even so, Strauch contends that Holden rejects adult materialism when he skips his coins into the lake, suggesting that he is resigned to leaving childhood behind but not prepared to accept the corruptions that adulthood represents.[46] The scenes at the family home with Phoebe are also pivotal: once Holden has remembered the fall of James Castle and expressed his desire to be a catcher, he escapes twice, from his home and then from Antolini. For Strauch, Holden is 'paradoxically headed for both physical capture and psychological escape'.[47]

Strauch believes that, to Holden, Jane and Allie (the former representing sex and the latter death) are linked: both have been taken from Holden and his insecurity stems from an overwhelming sense of loss. However, after Holden passes out in the museum there is an implication that he has come to terms with Allie's death: Holden 'is reborn into a new world of secure feelings and emotions, with himself fulfilling the office of catcher in his mature view of Phoebe'.[48] Phoebe plays a crucial role because she allows Holden both to remain a child through his relationship with her and to grow up by parenting her; this continuity between the roles of child and parent allows Holden to develop.

Throughout the essay Strauch identifies numerous telling details and interprets them with great imagination. A good example of this is his understanding of the significance of Holden's red hunting cap: 'The hat [. . .] is the central symbol of Holden's fantasy and so of the book' because it expresses Holden's anger (it is a people-shooting hat); it empowers him with a feeling of rebellion (it is the hat he wears to escape from school and pursue his quest around Manhattan); it is a catcher's hat (when worn with the peak around to the back) and so it fits with his fantasy of being a catcher in the rye.[49] Overall, Strauch maintains this same level of detail throughout his reading of the novel, creating a very interesting, occasionally quite difficult, and very imaginative interpretation that still stands as one of the major critical works.

Bernard Oldsey, writing in 1961, was interested in the significance of Hollywood film to the novel. Of course, it is not difficult to see that Holden has a contradictory attitude to 'the movies': he claims to hate them but has obviously seen many films and often invokes them when he is feeling playful (as when he mimics Fred Astaire for Stradlater) or distressed (his fantasy of being shot by and then shooting Maurice). However, Oldsey contends that Holden measures the

44 Strauch, 'Kings in the Back Row', p. 7.
45 Strauch, 'Kings in the Back Row', p. 19.
46 Strauch, 'Kings in the Back Row', p. 19.
47 Strauch, 'Kings in the Back Row', p. 20.
48 Strauch, 'Kings in the Back Row', p. 23.
49 Strauch, 'Kings in the Back Row', p. 16.

people he meets by the way in which they 'react to phoniness [. . .] especially cinematic': for example, he disparages the women he meets in the Lavender Room for their interest in film actors, Sunny's movie-going depresses him, and his brother D. B. is a 'prostitute' because he works in the film industry.[50] There is, then, a certain hypocrisy in Holden's attitude to cinema. Oldsey suggests that this is highlighted by the possibility that Salinger arrived at his protagonist's name by combining the names of two film stars: William Holden and Joan Caulfield, who starred together in a 1947 film, *Dear Ruth*.

For Oldsey it is significant that Phoebe, who represents the opposite of phony, is enthusiastic about the movies: Holden notes that her favourite film is *The 39 Steps* (1935) which she knows by heart. Phoebe offers Holden a detailed description of a film she has just seen, *The Doctor*, which is concerned with euthanasia. Oldsey considers this film to be emblematic of Holden's situation: the euthanasia theme is related to Holden's wish to save the young (from illness in the film and from loss of innocence in Holden's fantasy); for his actions, the doctor is imprisoned, while Holden is sent to an institution. Similarly, Oldsey connects Jane's experiences with her stepfather to a book and film titled *Kings Row* (1942), the link being suggested by Jane's strategy of hoarding her kings when playing checkers. Oldsey argues that '*Kings Row* shares with *The Catcher in the Rye* three notable elements: youthful innocence in a world of adult cruelty, possible confinement in a mental institution, and a muted theme of incest'.[51] Oldsey makes a strong case that the films discussed or alluded to in the novel make a significant contribution to our interpretation of the text. *The Doctor* suggests that if Holden pursues his plan to save the innocent he may suffer serious consequences, while *Kings Row* implies that Jane's relationship with her stepfather is damaging and incestuous.

Although Holden dreams of finding a way to escape the phoniness that he believes to be fundamentally connected to the corrupting influence of the movies, one of the ironies of the novel is that Holden tells his story from a location very near Hollywood. Oldsey's contention that we can find interesting implications not only in Holden's ambivalent attitude to the movies, but also in the way that certain films mirror or comment upon events in the novel, opens up new interpretive possibilities. Readers could go on to consider the significance of the protagonist desperately trying to escape in *The 39 Steps* or the uncertainties about identity in the film Holden watches at Radio City. Oldsey is not the first critic to see that Holden both loves and hates the movies, but his essay is the first to consider how *Catcher*'s film references may shape our interpretation.

In 1962 Brian Way published an essay on Salinger's *Franny and Zooey*, which he obviously disliked intensely. By contrast, Way considered *Catcher* to be 'the best novel published since the war' and his essay explains why he praises it so highly, offering useful insights into the novel.[52] Way identifies in *Catcher* what he calls a three-movement structure: 'The first movement shows Holden Caulfield at school; the second, his escape to New York and search there for sexual adventure; the third, his collapse, at the conscious level, backward into childhood, at the

50 Bernard S. Oldsey, 'The Movies in The Rye', in Joel Salzberg (ed.), *Critical Essays on Salinger's The Catcher in the Rye*, Boston, Mass.: G. K. Hall, 1990, p. 95.
51 Oldsey, 'The Movies in The Rye', p. 96.
52 Brian Way, ' "Franny and Zooey" and J. D. Salinger', *New Left Review*, May/June 1962, p. 74.

unconscious forward into madness.'[53] This proposal in itself may not break new ground, but what is interesting about Way's reading is its contention that the issue of adolescent sexuality is central to the novel.

Way considers the most successful part of the novel to be the second, which describes 'Holden's four successive attempts at sexual satisfaction' (calling Faith Cavendish, dancing with the women in the Lavender Room, Sunny the prostitute, the proposal to Sally Hayes).[54] Way believes that sex is a central issue in the novel, not least because Holden's fantasies are consistently undermined by the realities of his sexual encounters: 'In *The Catcher*, experience incapacitates and destroys, and after the failure of Holden's last attempt at satisfaction, he is moving towards mental collapse.'[55] So in this interpretation it is Holden's sexual experiences that determine what happens to him in the last section of the novel: ' "Sex," says Holden, "is something I just don't understand." From this flows everything.'[56]

Way likes the final part of the novel – Holden's collapse, including his visit to Phoebe – least of all. He finds Phoebe an unconvincing character, describing her as a 'miniature adult [. . .] detestable and unreal'; he considers the significance of her role in Holden's breakthrough to be undermined by the sentimentality of their relationship.[57] In Way's view, Salinger misrepresents the supposed innocence of children to create a 'rosy, sentimental, backward view of childhood' and believes that the novel does not actually support the interpretation that Holden craves a return to childhood.[58] For this critic, what is most interesting about the novel is what he reads as its realistic and unsentimental representation of the difficulties of coping with sexuality in adolescence; what is least interesting to him are the very scenes that most other critics praise (those between Holden and Phoebe). Way concludes that 'the novel's greatness is flawed by the denouement and rests on those earlier scenes of adolescence where there is no falsity of observation, lapse of consciousness, or failure of control'.[59]

Approaches to *Catcher* have certainly varied widely over the years. In 1966, for example, John M. Howell published an essay that likened *Catcher* to T. S. Eliot's poem *The Waste Land* (1922), going so far as to claim that Salinger found a 'controlling metaphor' for his novel in Eliot's famous poem. This reading is very complex: the parallels it identifies between poem and novel include the carrousel that Phoebe rides being like the Buddhist wheel of life and death; the frozen lake in Central Park being (like Eliot's frozen river Thames) a symbol of sterility; Allie's glove being 'a kind of spiritual gauntlet which Holden as "catcher" must carry into the waste land'.[60] Howell also makes many connections between characters in the poem and in the novel: James Castle is Jesus Christ (initials J. C.); Allie is Allah; Holden is Prince Ferdinand (he often calls people 'prince'); Mr Spencer is Madame Sosostris (both have bad colds and tell the future using Egyptian-related items: tarot cards and Holden's history exam paper). Like the

53 Way, 'Franny and Zooey', p. 75.
54 Way, 'Franny and Zooey', p. 77.
55 Way, 'Franny and Zooey', p. 77.
56 Way, 'Franny and Zooey', p. 78.
57 Way, 'Franny and Zooey', p. 81.
58 Way, 'Franny and Zooey', p. 81.
59 Way, 'Franny and Zooey', p. 82.
60 John M. Howell, 'Salinger in The Waste Land', in Joel Salzberg (ed.), *Critical Essays on Salinger's The Catcher in The Rye*, Boston, Mass.: G. K. Hall, 1990, p. 87.

comparisons with *Huckleberry Finn*, an interpretation of this sort places *Catcher* firmly into a respected literary tradition, but here it is not quite clear how the two texts, once connected, illuminate each other. Even so, Howell's analysis certainly testifies to the richness and potential of *Catcher* to provoke a range of possible interpretations.

By the time that Howell published his essay, academic interpretations of *Catcher* had hit a peak, and the backlash against both *Catcher* and its critics was also well under way. In 1959, before the novel was even ten years old, George Steiner had coined the phrase 'The Salinger Industry' to describe the outpouring of critical commentary on the author and, especially, on his most famous work. Steiner considers Salinger to be 'a good minor writer with an audience which is, by any traditional tokens, largely illiterate'.[61] He is scathing about Heiserman and Miller's likening of *Catcher* to classic quest narratives; he describes Holden as 'Salinger's young lout', a figure not meriting the comparisons critics had made between Holden and questing figures such as Ulysses, Gatsby, or Ishmael (of Melville's *Moby Dick*).[62] Steiner suggests that to be compared with *Huckleberry Finn* would be 'high praise for any modern novel' and that it is inappropriate to suggest, as Edgar Branch does, that *Catcher* is superior: Steiner deems this and other high praise of Salinger's work 'pomposities and exaggerations'.[63] Steiner concedes that Salinger is 'a gifted and entertaining writer with one excellent short novel and a number of memorable stories to his credit. [. . .] He has a marvellous ear for the semiliterate meanderings of the adolescent mind.'[64]

Although Steiner does not think Salinger untalented, he does suggest that his work is dangerous, in the sense that young readers may find in Holden a negative model, one that affirms their 'formal ignorance [and] political apathy' as 'positive virtues'.[65] Having disparaged the readers, Steiner goes on to attack the critics, suggesting that what he deems inappropriately hyperbolic praise of Salinger is simply a strategy that fulfils a desire in academic critics to write overly compli-cated textual analysis and an equally pressing need to find something new to write about. Steiner concludes that 'Of course, Salinger is a most skilful and original writer. Of course, he is worth discussing and praising. But not in terms appropriate to the master poets of the world.'[66]

In the same year, William Wiegand published an essay that could be read as a defence of Salinger's worth against critics like Steiner. For Wiegand, the author's popularity simply rests on his skill, especially in terms of his creation of characters that are 'so uncomfortably alive that one has a kind of irrational desire to keep after them and see if something can't be worked out'.[67] Wiegand sees Salinger as a writer committed to experimentation and offering readers a new, provocative kind of fiction that responds to contemporary concerns: his work 'answers a need for a different kind of treatment of experience'.[68] For this critic, these strengths

61 George Steiner, 'The Salinger Industry', *Nation*, 199, 1959, p. 360.
62 Steiner, 'The Salinger Industry', p. 361.
63 Steiner, 'The Salinger Industry', p. 361.
64 Steiner, 'The Salinger Industry', p. 361.
65 Steiner, 'The Salinger Industry', p. 362.
66 Steiner, 'The Salinger Industry', p. 363.
67 William Wiegand, 'The Knighthood of J. D. Salinger', *New Republic*, 141, 1959, p. 19.
68 Wiegand, 'The Knighthood of J. D. Salinger', p. 21.

explain the popularity that Steiner finds so inexplicable. However, two years later, Alfred Kazin comments scathingly that Salinger has acquired a vast readership by flattering those who 'think of themselves as endlessly sensitive, spiritually alone, gifted, and whose suffering lies in the narrowing of their consciousness to themselves, in the withdrawal of their curiosity from a society which they think they understand too well'.[69] The implication is that Salinger is affirming the validity of feelings that Kazin obviously considers unjustifiable and indulgent and, because Salinger's readers tend to be young people, this may even be irresponsible.

The year 1961 also saw the appearance of two defences of *Catcher*. Robert Gutwillig contends that although 'There has never been a more "American" novel than *The Catcher in the Rye*', it has been translated into several languages, affirming that it is simply a 'literary phenomena of the first order'.[70] *Catcher* is a success because it offers readers 'the shock and thrill of recognition' and a sense of involvement with its narrator: when Holden comments on the scene with Phoebe at the carrousel, 'I wish you could have been there', Gutwillig says, 'We are there.'[71] Gutwillig's praise, because it rests on affinity between reader and narrator, assumes that the two are very similar: *Catcher*'s typical reader must be a young, white, educated, middle-class male, like Holden himself. Since this description also applies to most members of the critical establishment and university faculties – especially during the 1950s and 1960s – it took a surprisingly long time for the realisation to dawn that, in fact, Holden does not represent all adolescents: to believe that he does is to accept a myth created by the dominance of conventional power structures related to race, gender and class. More recent essays on the novel, including the new readings offered in the next chapter (see Critical readings, **pp. 67–118**) do challenge such ideas. There is, however, little evidence of such consideration in the essays of this earlier period, other than comments by Anne Marple, who notices that women tend to play one of two roles in Salinger's fiction ('insensitive girlfriend' or 'shallow wife'), and Leslie Fiedler who contends that 'Salinger, of course, speaks for the cleanest, politest, best-dressed, best-fed and best-read among the disaffected young'.[72] Even so, neither critic makes these observations central to their discussion of Salinger's work.

Edward Corbett's 1961 defence of *Catcher* is an attempt to ward off censors rather than critics. Efforts to ban *Catcher* offer another link with *Huckleberry Finn*, which has also faced censorship at various times (see Texts and contexts, **pp. 17–19**). It is no coincidence that both novels are concerned with young people and often read by them, even if they were not the original target audience. Corbett concedes that 'Considered in isolation, the language *is* crude and profane', but he argues that the swearing is essential to the 'integrity of the novel' and that its inclusion does not guarantee that the book will corrupt readers.[73] Amusingly, Corbett contends that teenage girls find Holden's language unconvincing because

69 Alfred Kazin, 'J. D. Salinger: Everybody's Favourite', *Atlantic Monthly*, 208, 1961, p. 31.
70 Robert Gutwillig, 'Everybody's Caught *The Catcher in the Rye*', *New York Times Book Review*, 15 January 1961, p. 38.
71 Gutwillig, 'Everybody's Caught *The Catcher in the Rye*', p. 39.
72 Anne Marple, 'Salinger's Oasis of Innocence', *New Republic*, 145, 1961, p. 23; Leslie Fiedler, 'Up from Adolescence', *Partisan Review*, 29, 1962, p. 128.
73 Edward Corbett, 'Raise High the Barriers, Censors: Some Thoughts on *The Catcher in the Rye*', *America*, 104, 1961, pp. 441, 442.

teenage boys are so gentlemanly that they 'temper their language' in the company of girls.[74] As to the novel's 'scandalous' episodes, Corbett contends that 'no novel is immoral merely because vice is represented in it', arguing that Holden may be involved in shocking activities (engaging a prostitute being the key example) but his responses to these situations – of discomfort, even fear – show that he is a moral character at heart.[75] Holden may tell lies but he is not a phony; although troubled, he has 'a solid substratum of goodness, genuineness and sensitivity' and is therefore not a poor role model.[76] Echoing some of the novel's earliest reviews, Corbett concludes that *Catcher* is not 'an immoral, corrupting book [but] a subtle, sophisticated novel that requires an experienced, mature reader'.[77]

'Poised between two worlds': criticism of the 1970s and 1980s

It is probably inevitable that the surge of *Catcher* criticism that began in the late 1950s would lose some of its momentum; after all, what could possibly be left to say about the novel? However, critical perspectives change as time passes and, over the next twenty years, analysis of *Catcher* was dominated by new ways of reading informed by Marxist and psychoanalytic theory. Although some critics continued to follow established lines of enquiry (comparing Holden to Fyodor Dostoyevsky's narrator in *Notes from Underground* and Dickens's *David Copperfield*, for example, or reading the novel for its potential insights into an adolescent perspective), Marxism and psychoanalysis were the two key critical tools of the period. Interestingly, both Marxist and psychoanalytical perspectives generated more than a series of essays on *Catcher*: critics engaged in dialogue over what they considered to be misreadings of the novel, creating a critical debate that was more focused than it had ever been before. In this section, the Marxist debate will be explored first, followed by the psychoanalytic; the latter, in fact, spills over into the final section of this chapter.

Both theories are complex, with long histories and a variety of perspectives developing from central concepts. Marxist literary criticism has at its heart an interest in the relationship between the texts that a culture produces and the ideologies that lie beneath that culture. In Marxist terms, ideology is always driven by economic forces (the 'base') and so a society's 'superstructure' (its art, philosophy, novels and so on) must be interpreted in relation to the impact of economic forces and the inequalities these inevitably produce in a hierarchical system. Thus, a Marxist literary critic will be interested in the ways in which a novel represents the dominance of one social class over another, whether it affirms or resists that dominance and whether the values of the empowered classes are treated as ideal or problematic. Psychoanalytic literary criticism is comparable to Marxist criticism in the sense that both apply to texts theoretical perspectives that first developed in relation to other concerns: Marxism is an economic and

---

74 Corbett, 'Raise High the Barriers, Censors', p. 442.
75 Corbett, 'Raise High the Barriers, Censors', p. 442.
76 Corbett, 'Raise High the Barriers, Censors', p. 443.
77 Corbett, 'Raise High the Barriers, Censors', p. 443.

political theory which contends that such fundamental aspects of society have an impact on its culture, while psychoanalysis has been developing since the late nineteenth century as a way of understanding the relationship between human experience and behaviour. Psychoanalysis is an umbrella term for a range of theoretical perspectives that may be applied to texts in order to interpret characters, plot, language and form. Such an analysis is principally based on an understanding of the relationship between conscious and unconscious aspects of the mind, the latter being the aspect that drives behaviours and responses to experience in ways that are beyond an individual's control. Originally used as a way of understanding an author's motivations, psychoanalytic criticism in its various forms is now more often applied to a text's language to illuminate aspects of its characters, plot and theme.

Social change both drives and reflects changes in theoretical perspective. For example, some critics have praised *Catcher* for what they see as its 'universal' qualities, meaning that key aspects of Holden's experience will be shared by the majority of other people. Another way of understanding this claim is that critics who are in many ways adult versions of Holden in terms of their gender, class and race perceive in Holden a character who represents themselves and therefore – they assume – represents everyone. Developments in critical thinking since the 1970s have made it increasingly difficult for any critic to use a term like 'universal', because the possibility that there can be such a thing as a universal experience in a diverse world now seems untenable, and so it is equally unlikely that any novel could represent a universal experience. Indeed, the concept of 'universality' raises important issues because it reveals that those in powerful social positions assume the right to decide what is true for everyone else; anyone who fails to conform to the dominant model is 'Other', subordinate in a hierarchical social structure that confers privilege based on issues such as gender, race and class.

By 1976, when the critical team Carol and Richard Ohmann published their essay on *Catcher*, the novel had sold 9 million copies in the USA; there was no doubt that it was both a best-seller and a classic. The Ohmanns, however, counter existing criticism by refuting the conventional view that *Catcher*'s success rests in its representation of adolescence as an experience recognisable to any reader. On the contrary, they argue that Holden is a character who is profoundly linked to a specific historical moment (1951) and place (New York) and is a representative of bourgeois (privileged middle-class) social status. However, they do not see this as a flaw in *Catcher*. Instead, they believe that the flaw lies in critical essays that fail to notice this aspect of the novel, which they consider to be central to its success. Existing criticism treats the novel as if it is unconnected to its social or political context: critics focus on its relationship to other fictions and literary genres or, if they relate the novel to 'life', it is life only as they narrowly understand it. This strategy 'blurs and mutes' the analysis of a novel which, to the Ohmanns, is 'precisely revealing of social relationships in mid-century America, and motives that sustain them, and rationalizations that mask them'.[78]

Interpreting the novel divorced from the context of its time and place means

---

78 Carol Ohmann and Richard Ohmann, 'Reviewers, Critics, and *The Catcher in the Rye*', in Salzberg, *Critical Essays*, p. 122. First published in *Critical Inquiry*, 3, 1976, pp. 15–37.

that critics attribute Holden's troubles to one of two issues: either he is dealing with an inner struggle or he is at odds with the outside world. The Ohmanns contend that the 'inner struggle' model takes no account of Holden's context, while the 'outside world' model – which might seem to be interested in context – is considered by earlier critics only in very broad terms, such as 'evil', 'immorality', and 'corruption'. Even when Holden's problems are located in modern American society, critics still 'tend away from precise description of the society Salinger renders in *Catcher*'.[79] The Ohmanns believe that all of this vagueness 'work[s] to obscure how much Salinger did represent of the contemporary world in *Catcher*, and how far he understood what he represented'.[80] Rejecting the large concepts that other critics have chosen, the Ohmanns argue for precise analysis rooted in details: 'Holden lives in a time and place, and these provide the material against which his particular adolescent sensibility reacts.'[81]

As Marxist critics, the Ohmanns find a great deal of material in *Catcher* that they read as evidence of Salinger's awareness of class inequality, social hypocrisy and the impact of capitalism. A concrete example of this is Holden's description of his relationship with Dick Slagle, a friendship that was spoiled because the class barrier that separated the two boys could not be crossed. Holden would like to be friends with Dick: they are equals in intelligence and share a sense of humour. However, the novel recognises that objects as mundane as suitcases communicate that the boys live in a society in which Holden belongs to the strata of privilege and Dick does not, and they both know it. While Dick would like to belong, he recognises that the class he aspires to join positions him as inferior; this recognition inevitably causes him to hate Holden, who represents the superior social position that affluence allows.[82] The fact that Holden is saddened by this situation indicates the political intentions of the novel, which critiques capitalism for the damage it inflicts on social relations. Thus, the Ohmanns contend, comments about the novel that universalise its meaning are in error, because 'they displace the political emotion that is an important part of [*Catcher*], finding causes for it that are presumed to be universal'.[83] Equally, critics' ideas about what Holden yearns for are often based around an archetypal search for self and have at their foundation a set of assumptions about an innate, universally agreed concept of what it means to be 'human'.

It is clear from the novel that Holden likes people who challenge convention such as Allie, Jane, Richard Kinsella (who digressed), James Castle, the nuns, the museum (which defies change): 'For Holden, images of the valuable are generally images of people withdrawn from convention – people who are private, whimsical, losers, saints, dead.'[84] Despite all his plans, Holden does not escape but settles for the society he has. Encouraged by the example of Phoebe and changed by his experiences, he becomes more accepting of his society and by the end of the novel he even feels nostalgic for people and prospects that he previously disparaged. For the Ohmanns, all of this proves that:

79 Ohmann and Ohmann, in Salzberg, *Critical Essays*, p. 127.
80 Ohmann and Ohmann, in Salzberg, *Critical Essays*, p. 128.
81 Ohmann and Ohmann, in Salzberg, *Critical Essays*, p. 129.
82 Ohmann and Ohmann, in Salzberg, *Critical Essays*, p. 133.
83 Ohmann and Ohmann, in Salzberg, *Critical Essays*, p. 132.
84 Ohmann and Ohmann, in Salzberg, *Critical Essays*, p. 135.

The Catcher in the Rye is among other things a serious critical mimesis [representation] of bourgeois life in the Eastern United States, ca. 1950 – of snobbery, privilege, class injury, culture as a badge of superiority, sexual exploitation, education subordinated to status, warped social feeling, competitiveness, stunted human possibility [. . .] Salinger is astute in imagining these hurtful things, though not in explaining them.[85]

Far from being buried in the novel, the Ohmanns contend that these themes are 'central to the book's meaning'.[86] While Holden is an engaging, sensitive and observant character, 'he is an adolescent with a limited understanding of what he perceives'; adult readers, however, have a clearer understanding and can see that Holden's unconventional values are incompatible with the society in which he lives. Advanced capitalism, which is so central to modern American society, creates the illusion that everyone can prosper and so it feeds the desire for prosperity while actually inhibiting the attainment of that desire, because general prosperity undermines capitalism. The few prosper at the expense of the many and close their eyes to the reality of this inequality so that they can enjoy what they have. Recognising the importance of this in *Catcher* allows the Ohmanns to conclude that the 'force of the novel is quite precisely located in its rendering a contradiction of a particular society, as expressed through an adolescent sensibility that feels, though it cannot comprehend, this contradiction'.[87] In essence, it is the particularity of the novel that makes it a successful (and politically aware) novel, not its universality. This response to the novel is very engaging and credible and presents a significant challenge to existing criticism. This challenge was not left unanswered for long.

James Miller – the same critic who wrote the first comparison of *Catcher* and *Huckleberry Finn* in 1956 (see Critical history, **p. 47**) – describes the Ohmanns' reading as 'comprehensive and exclusive', meaning that they cover the whole of the novel and their interpretation leaves no room for other perspectives: agreeing with them means that 'other views [. . .] are no longer tenable'.[88] Miller finds the Ohmanns' reading 'simplistic' because of its basis in a critique of capitalist values: 'To see Holden's malaise of spirit solely or even mainly caused by the evils of a capitalistic society is surely myopic [. . .] Holden's sickness of soul is something deeper than economic or political.'[89] A Marxist critic might well respond that there is nothing deeper than the economic or political and that these are more than able to sicken a soul. However, aside from the unusual reading that Holden's encounter with Maurice is the novel's 'important comic scene', much of Miller's challenge to the Ohmanns is familiar from earlier criticism (exactly the perspectives they aimed to challenge).[90] These include asserting that Holden is both envious of and protective towards children as he struggles to come to terms with

---

85 Ohmann and Ohmann, in Salzberg, *Critical Essays*, p. 135.
86 Ohmann and Ohmann, in Salzberg, *Critical Essays*, p. 136.
87 Ohmann and Ohmann, in Salzberg, *Critical Essays*, p. 136.
88 James E. Miller, '*Catcher* In and Out of History', in Salzberg, *Critical Essays*, p. 141. First published in *Critical Inquiry*, 3, 1977, pp. 599–603.
89 Miller, in Salzberg, *Critical Essays*, pp. 141–2.
90 Miller, in Salzberg, *Critical Essays*, p. 142.

adult sexuality; that the figure of Antolini is important and there is doubt over his motives; that Holden faces death in the Egyptian tomb and then decides to 'rejoin the human race' when he watches Phoebe on the carrousel and realises that he cannot shield her from painful experiences but he can enjoy her innocent pleasure in life.[91] In this way, Miller contends, Holden is reconciled to his society, and this is not – as the Ohmanns argue – a shortcoming of the novel: 'The Ohmanns might have recognised that Holden has been awakened to a precondition of a better society – love of fellow human beings – before condemning Salinger for not instilling Holden with a vision of the kind of ideal state that has never existed before and seems not to exist now.'[92] This final point does not seem to take into account that, if the Ohmanns condemn anybody, it is the critics for misreading the novel, not Salinger for failing to write the novel they wished for; indeed, they praise the novel highly.

When the Ohmanns respond to Miller, they observe that he is inclined to universalise, a critical strategy they find problematic. They suggest that Miller's approach is narrow and that he presents his critical methodology as if it were 'the critical methodology', which is very much what he accused them of doing; his limited perspective 'implies a reading of history, and that reading amounts to a denial that history happens'.[93] They contend that 'literature both reflects and helps to create historical change': for example, adolescence in the post-war American sense is not a feature of English medieval literature, because in the medieval period youth was celebrated and perceptions of young people were very different from the 1950s definition of a teenager.[94] Writing about adolescence reflects the society it comes from, and the society of post-war America was especially conscious of the significance of an identifiable developmental period between childhood and adulthood. So *Catcher*, the Ohmanns claim, is obviously a product of the concerns of its moment because Holden's anxieties about sex, death, injustice and so on 'are embedded in his full experience of society'.[95]

The Ohmanns go on to offer a range of interesting examples that support their central contention that the novel represents – and critiques – Holden's time and place, essentially through Holden's rejection of the choices his society offers him to express his masculinity through social climbing, sexual aggression and antipathy towards homosexuals. When Miller claims that Holden's experiences are evidence of 'unchanging human nature', the Ohmanns claim that he is utilising 'a special vocabulary of bourgeois thought' that refuses to acknowledge (because it does not suit it to do so) that the societies we live in are 'changeable and historically defined'.[96] Ultimately, for the Ohmanns, the interpretation offered by Miller and any other critic who deploys 'universals' rather than taking account of political, historical and social significance is inadequate because such a reading 'rests on a scheme of history that will not stand up to scrutiny', a scheme that is

91 Miller, in Salzberg, *Critical Essays*, p. 143.
92 Miller, in Salzberg, *Critical Essays*, p. 143.
93 Carol Ohmann and Richard Ohmann, 'Universals and the Historically Particular', in Salzberg *Critical Essays*, p. 145. First published in *Critical Inquiry*, 3, 1977, pp. 773–7.
94 Ohmann and Ohmann, in Salzberg, *Critical Essays*, p. 145.
95 Ohmann and Ohmann, in Salzberg, *Critical Essays*, p. 145.
96 Ohmann and Ohmann, in Salzberg, *Critical Essays*, p. 146.

bourgeois and irresponsible because it tries to obscure the precise critique of society that a novel like *Catcher* offers.[97]

Like Marxist analysis, psychoanalytic criticism has implications for the ways in which texts of all kinds can be read. Because the broad term 'psychoanalysis' encompasses a range of theoretical perspectives, psychoanalytic interpretations of *Catcher* often disagree with each other and provoke debate amongst critics. Some of the most provocative readings of the novel have come from psychoanalytic critics and, while readers may disagree with their point of view, they certainly offer new ways of thinking about the novel.

James Bryan's essay 'The Psychological Structure of *The Catcher in the Rye*' begins with a fairly uncontroversial assertion of the centrality to the plot of Holden's developing sexuality, much as Brian Way did in his 1962 essay (see Critical history, **pp. 46–7**). Bryan suggests that Holden is preoccupied with sex (which he associates with adult callousness) and with children (whom he associates with innocence); it is the ways in which these two preoccupations coincide that interests Bryan. In New York, Holden is bombarded with sexual matters (seen from the hotel window, the scene with Sunny, the 'fuck you' graffiti) many of them also associated with death, such as the man who touches his girlfriend intimately while discussing suicide and the magazine Holden reads after he has run away from Antolini, which convinces him he is ill.[98] One interpretation of the impact of these events on Holden is that they strengthen his desire to protect children from similar experiences, but Bryan takes a different view when he suggests that 'the urgency of Holden's compulsions, his messianic desire to guard innocence against adult corruption [. . .] comes of a frantic need to save his sister from himself'.[99]

Bryan believes that Holden is going through a process of sexual maturing that leads him to focus sexually on first his mother, then his sister, then finally on other women. At the moment in which we meet him in the novel, his sexual desire is focused on Phoebe, a desire that fuses his need for innocence with his adult urges. He wants to protect Phoebe from the loss of innocence and changes that may be imposed upon her by his complex desires. Bryan's evidence to support this interpretation includes the fact that Holden describes Phoebe as 'too affectionate', as if physical contact with her makes him uncomfortable. Bryan also notes that Holden is more attracted to Bernice (from the Lavender Room) once he has likened her to Phoebe and that he perceives Sunny the prostitute to be childlike, which troubles him.[100]

For Bryan, Holden's inability to have a sexual relationship with a girl his own age is explained by 'his confused feelings about Phoebe'.[101] When Holden visits Phoebe in her bedroom, 'double entendres and sexually suggestive images and gestures multiply', including discarded clothes and the comment that Holden feels 'swell', as if sexually aroused.[102] Oldsey (see Critical history, **pp. 45–6**) considers

97 Ohmann and Ohmann, in Salzberg, *Critical Essays*, p. 147.
98 James Bryan, 'The Psychological Structure of *The Catcher in the Rye*', in Salzberg, *Critical Essays*, p. 105. First published in *PMLA*, 89, 1974, pp. 1065–74.
99 Bryan, in Salzberg, *Critical Essays*, p. 107.
100 Bryan, in Salzberg, *Critical Essays*, p. 108.
101 Bryan, in Salzberg, *Critical Essays*, p. 110.
102 Bryan, in Salzberg, *Critical Essays*, p. 110.

that the significance of the film about euthanasia that Phoebe describes is that Holden, like the doctor, wishes to save children. However, Bryan maintains that it implies that Holden may 'kill' Phoebe psychologically with sexually inappropriate behaviour. He contends that Holden can't answer Phoebe's question about naming something he likes because 'the truth' – his desire for Phoebe – is 'too close'.[103] Holden's fantasy of being a catcher in the rye is based on a song he has misremembered and it is Phoebe who reminds him that the song is a romance. Bryan contends that Holden's inaccurate memory of the song is significant: 'Because he has to, Holden has substituted a messianic motive for the true, erotic one', meaning that Holden claims to want the role of protector when his intentions – which his unconscious represses – are actually sexual.[104]

Bryan contends that Holden's response to the scene with Antolini 'may torment him most for its parallels to his own unconscious designs on a child'.[105] His panic about Antolini, along with his 'unfounded suspicions' about Jane's stepfather and his anger towards the 'perverty bum' who wrote 'fuck you' on the school wall are reflections of Holden's own fears about himself.[106] These episodes are followed by increased fantasies of disappearing and escape, and Holden's anger at Phoebe when she pleads to escape with him is driven by the fact that it is actually Phoebe he wants to escape from. Holden's rejection of Phoebe as a partner, someone he could escape with, signals the end of their relationship as 'lovers' and allows them to reunite as brother and sister.[107] Watching Phoebe on the carrousel, Holden finds a 'mature, new perspective' and sees that she must be allowed to find her own way.[108] This last part of the analysis, at least, does not conflict with other critics' interpretations. However, much of Bryan's reading of Holden's motivations in the novel, while innovative, is likely to shock many readers, particularly those who identify with Holden as a character. As with the work by the Ohmanns, Bryan's interpretation provoked a direct response from another critic.

Dennis Vail takes issue with Bryan on several counts, not least his reading – or, as Vail terms it, 'misreading' – of Holden's relationship with Phoebe. For Vail, the novel's strength is that it suggests it is possible to have meaningful relationships that are not based in sex, as Holden does with Phoebe and with Jane: 'Such contact need *not* be corrupt.'[109] Vail believes that such relationships issue a challenge to the 'you' that the narrative is addressed to, someone who may see sexual corruption where there is actually innocence. If Holden exploits Phoebe at all, it is by taking her Christmas money, and he only needs it because he has himself been exploited in a more overtly sexual context by Sunny's pimp, Maurice.

Vail contends that it is the non-sexual relationship that Holden shares with Phoebe that creates his salvation and that he, in turn, protects Phoebe, taking responsibility for her by giving her his red hat. She forces him to reject his escapist

103 Bryan, in Salzberg, *Critical Essays*, p. 111.
104 Bryan, in Salzberg, *Critical Essays*, p. 112.
105 Bryan, in Salzberg, *Critical Essays*, p. 114.
106 Bryan, in Salzberg, *Critical Essays*, p. 114.
107 Bryan, in Salzberg, *Critical Essays*, p. 115.
108 Bryan, in Salzberg, *Critical Essays*, p. 115.
109 Dennis Vail, 'Holden and Psychoanalysis', in Salzberg, *Critical Essays*, p. 117. First published in *PMLA*, 91, 1976, pp. 120–1.

fantasies by asking him to consider what he likes and to recognise the impossibility of running away; the validity of her perspective causes him to be angry with her.
The novel contains recurring images of falling, which symbolize both falling from
life into death (as Allie and James Castle have done) and from innocence into
corruption (as D. B. has done and Phoebe may do). Antolini fears that Holden too
will fall (into corruption) and Holden himself fears that he will die. Because the
novel associates sex with corruption, and corruption with death, the novel asserts
a relationship between sex and death.[110] So, far from Holden being corrupt and
threatening to (sexually) corrupt Phoebe, Vail maintains that both characters are
innocents who allow the reader to understand the novel's central message, which
is that:

> Maintaining one's essential innocence in full knowledge of and contact
> with an essentially corrupt world [. . .] constitutes the only maturity
> worth having. It is this that promises to flower in Phoebe and that
> Holden himself finally shows promise of being able to achieve. It is rare
> [. . .] But nothing less is acceptable [. . .] Everything else is death.[111]

Vail's refutation of Bryan's reading is offered in general terms: he recognises that
sex plays a part in the novel in that it represents the perils of adult society, but he
asserts that the loving relationship between Holden and Phoebe is an innocent
counter to the corrupting potential of sexual exploitation and that the novel is
essentially hopeful.

In contrast to Vail, Duane Edwards offers a reading of *Catcher* that once again
understands Holden to be a sexual figure: a repressed homosexual. Edwards
contends that Holden has 'voyeuristic tendencies': he looks rather than acts
because he is sexually shy, a shyness that stems from his 'unconscious desire' for
the same sex.[112] Edwards notes that Holden almost never manages to phone
women (especially not Jane), but he manages to phone Carl Luce and Mr Antolini,
both of whom could be read as homosexual: '*He* [Holden] seeks *them* out; he is
the aggressor if there is one.'[113] During his conversation with Luce, Holden
focuses on Luce's sexual activities and tells him 'I got a flit for you', which
Edwards reads as an attempt to 'make sexual contact' with Luce.[114] Holden has
already established that he likes older women (Mrs Morrow, for example) so
it is telling that Luce and Antolini have also formed relationships with women
older than themselves; this detail aligns Holden with these sexually ambiguous
characters.

Holden reacts so strongly to Antolini touching him because 'he is projecting
his desire for homosexual expression onto Antolini'.[115] Holden's desires are
unconscious (he does not understand why he 'is attracted to – and attracts –

---

110 Vail, in Salzberg, *Critical Essays*, p. 118.
111 Vail, in Salzberg, *Critical Essays*, p. 119.
112 Duane Edwards, 'Holden Caulfield: "Don't Ever Tell Anybody Anything"', in Salzberg, *Critical Essays*, p. 153. First Published in *English Literary History*, 44, 1977, pp. 554–65.
113 Edwards, in Salzberg, *Critical Essays*, p. 153.
114 Edwards, in Salzberg, *Critical Essays*, p. 153.
115 Edwards, in Salzberg, *Critical Essays*, p. 154.

homosexuals') but the scene with Antolini causes him to panic.[116] This terror is expressed in an outbreak of hypochondria and Holden's dream of escape into a world in which he lives as a deaf mute with a deaf-mute wife, away from men and unable to hear or speak to them. Edwards concludes that when critics read Holden's sentimentality as his expression of love, what they fail to see is that his over-romanticising is 'a symptom of his inability to express his feelings easily and naturally'.[117] Holden, then, is a character who fears his own desires so much that he has completely repressed them and his fascination with looking is a symptom of his consequent inability to connect intimately with another person.

R. J. Huber's 1984 essay on *Catcher* approaches it from a different psycho-analytical perspective, one based on the theories of Alfred Adler, the theorist most famous for originating the concept of 'inferiority' and 'superiority' complexes. Adler believes that human beings are always striving for 'completion' and, because completion is impossible to attain, humans are permanently in a state of 'becoming' rather than 'being'. Huber's essay offers some introductory material on Adler's theories and then applies them to an analysis of Holden. Adler believes that an individual's world view gives direction to his/her striving and shapes his/her perception of events; for Adler an individual cannot be explained but can 'only be understood by accurately assessing his or her world view. Literature, similarly, is not to be explained; it is to be understood from the psychological viewpoint of its characters'.[118] So for an Adlerian, understanding a real person or a fictional character is achieved by 'keen observation of behavioural minutiae to understand the individual's frame of reference'.[119] Such understanding allows the formation of a 'consistent psychological depiction', which is what Huber attempts to offer in this essay.[120]

Huber notes the longevity of Holden's appeal as a character, recognising that he is an 'adolescent folk hero' to many readers.[121] However, Huber doubts that Holden is really a typical adolescent: to an Adlerian, 'Holden is more prototypical of maladjustment in general than of normal adolescence. [He has] deep-seated inferiority feelings and a compensatory striving for grandiosity.'[122] Sometimes Holden's perceptions are correct – he 'aptly describes flaws in our society' – but 'Holden selectively attends to and retains the negative aspects of his world, and then depreciates others and his surroundings in order to compensate for deep-seated feelings of inferiority'.[123] The terms that Holden uses to describe himself do suggest that he considers himself to be inferior: even his sense that he is falling and his fear of disappearing can be interpreted as 'indicative of his intense feeling of failure and inferiority'.[124]

Holden has what Huber terms a 'yes-but' attitude to women: 'yes' is the goal

116 Edwards, in Salzberg, *Critical Essays*, p. 154.
117 Edwards, in Salzberg, *Critical Essays*, p. 155.
118 R. J. Huber, 'Adlerian Theory and its Application to *The Catcher in the Rye*: Holden Caulfield', in Joseph Natoli (ed.), *Psychological Perspectives on Literature: Freudian Dissidents and Non-Freudians: A Casebook*, Hamden, Conn.: Archon, 1984, p. 47.
119 Huber, in Natoli, *Psychological Perspectives on Literature*, p. 47.
120 Huber, in Natoli, *Psychological Perspectives on Literature*, p. 47.
121 Huber, in Natoli, *Psychological Perspectives on Literature*, p. 48.
122 Huber, in Natoli, *Psychological Perspectives on Literature*, p. 48.
123 Huber, in Natoli, *Psychological Perspectives on Literature*, p. 48.
124 Huber, in Natoli, *Psychological Perspectives on Literature*, p. 49.

while 'but' is the excuse for not achieving it.[125] His attitude to other people is similarly extreme: he sees himself as existing in 'enemy territory' and his disparaging response to society is a way for him to reassure himself that he is better than it. His fantasies, in which he plays out masculine roles that he has learned from the movies, are a product of these anxieties about his inferiority: when his 'grandiose self-image is threatened, he imagines himself as a dying hero'.[126] Holden's fantasies of stereotypical masculinity increase his sense of personal worth, an act Huber identifies as 'masculine protest', which means safeguarding self-esteem by being a 'real man'. Holden's 'repetitive use of profanity' is one sign of Holden's masculine protest, as are his constant offers to buy people drinks and his decision to engage a prostitute.[127] Holden's dream of being the catcher in the rye is one of 'useless grandiosity' in which he pictures himself as a god or saviour, again in an attempt to counter his belief in his actual inferiority.[128]

As with the Marxist and other psychoanalytic readings discussed here, Huber's essay offers a fresh and interesting perspective on a novel that was by the time of writing more than thirty years old. None of these essays offers a definitive analysis of the text: it will never be possible to identify the 'truth' of the novel, because no such single truth exists. One of the greatest strengths of fiction is that the same text can support many different readings, some of which may be in direct opposition to each other. Such a variety of interpretations allows the reader to make her or his own decisions about the possible meanings in a text. New readings are always possible, as the material discussed in this chapter – and the essays in Critical readings (pp. 67–118) – proves beyond doubt.

'A classic American hero'?: criticism from the 1990s to the present

In recent years, critical essays on *Catcher* have appeared regularly, following much the same pattern as that of the 1970s and 1980s in the sense that a few key essays break new ground while others – although not unoriginal – follow a more conventional pattern of relating the novel to other works of fiction or familiar themes. For the first time, however, essays express awareness that *Catcher* is now quite an old novel; indeed, many critics refer to the fact that the text has attained its fortieth or fiftieth anniversary as they write. Critics no longer need to wonder whether *Catcher* is an important novel – its place in the American canon is by now assured – but there is a sense in several essays that critics in this period feel an obligation to reflect on *Catcher*'s contribution to culture and society. Indeed, some essays are driven specifically by an urge to assess, as one title has it, 'Holden Caulfield's Legacy', or another, '*The Catcher in the Rye* and what It Spawned'.[129]

125 Huber, in Natoli, *Psychological Perspectives on Literature*, p. 50.
126 Huber, in Natoli, *Psychological Perspectives on Literature*, p. 50.
127 Huber, in Natoli, *Psychological Perspectives on Literature*, p. 51.
128 Huber, in Natoli, *Psychological Perspectives on Literature*, p. 51.
129 David Castronovo, 'Holden Caulfield's Legacy', *New England Review*, 22, 2001, pp. 180–6; Louis Menand, 'Holden at Fifty: *The Catcher in the Rye* and what It Spawned', *New Yorker*, 77, 2001, pp. 82–7.

Another new development in this period is the publication of anthologies of essays about Salinger and his work that offer personal reflections on the significance of the fiction for readers of all ages.[130] Volumes gathering together new and existing criticism appear more often now than they have since the heyday of *Catcher* criticism, some prefacing new essays with a brief critical overview, others reprinting 'classic' essays. All this activity could be read in two opposing ways: either that, since forty years have passed without Salinger publishing any new fiction, it is reasonable to see his life's work as complete and therefore available for what Steiner called 'final estimation'. The alternative viewpoint is that continued critical activity on *Catcher* simply demonstrates its inexhaustible capacity to inspire readers and critics, even ones very far removed from the time and place that produced the novel.

James Mellard adds his contribution to the field of psychoanalytical *Catcher* criticism with a reading based on the theories of psychoanalyst Jacques Lacan. This is a complex and challenging essay that includes a substantial amount of background material on 'Lacanian' theory, which has at its foundation the concept that when a child acquires language, she or he moves from the 'imaginary' (and identification with the mother) into the 'symbolic' (and the realm of the father) to become a mature subject. In response to critic James Bryan's assertion (see Critical history, **pp. 55–6**) that Holden desires Phoebe, Mellard argues that actually Holden has positioned Phoebe in the place of the mother, as the 'other' against which he defines himself as a subject. In order to enter the symbolic, Holden must 'resolve the Imaginary identification with this and additional types of others – "doubles" such as Ackley and Stradlater – in order to incorporate the role made for him in the Symbolic, a role that is located in the place of the father, but that is not specifically *his* father's place'.[131] In Lacanian terms, that is, taking the place of the father does not mean literally replacing the father (or symbolically 'killing' the father in the sense of Sigmund Freud's theory of the Oedipal Complex) but accepting the responsibilities of adulthood. For any developing person 'becoming an adult means accepting one's place in the structure where the mature subject stands', because it is this development that will allow a person to become 'a fully realized *subject*'.[132] So Mellard disagrees with those readings of the novel that see Holden's problems as primarily sexual and argues instead that 'it is mature *subjectivity*, not sexuality as such, that is Holden's problem'.[133]

Mellard uses Lacanian theory very directly in his interpretation of those moments in the novel in which Holden feels that he is disappearing. He contends that Holden's problem is recognised by Lacan as a symptom of his struggle to become a mature subject: 'disappearing' (termed *aphanisis* by Lacan) is specifically 'the "movement of disappearance" that the subject perceives at the advent of mature or Oedipal-stage subjectivity'.[134] It is significant that Holden first notices

130 Kip Kotzen and Thomas Beller (eds), *With Love and Squalor: 14 Writers Respond to the Work of J. D. Salinger*, New York: Broadway Books, 2001; Chris Kubica and Will Hochman (eds), *Letters to J. D. Salinger*, Madison, Wisc.: University of Wisconsin Press, 2002.
131 James M. Mellard, 'The Disappearing Subject: A Lacanian Reading of *The Catcher in the Rye*' in Salzberg, *Critical Essays*, p. 198.
132 Mellard, in Salzberg, *Critical Essays*, pp. 198, 199.
133 Mellard, in Salzberg, *Critical Essays*, p. 199.
134 Mellard, in Salzberg, *Critical Essays*, p. 199.

the feeling of disappearing on his way to see the ill and elderly Mr Spencer, who Holden sees as near death: throughout the novel Holden's thoughts about disappearing 'are related to those frequent ones about death and suicide'.[135] For example, Holden persistently worries about the fate of the ducks in Central Park and Mellard contends that Holden's concern about the ducks is related to his concerns about himself.[136] He wonders whether the ducks die when they disappear in winter and, towards the end of Chapter 20, Holden's thoughts move from the absence of the ducks, to his own death, to Allie's death. A Lacanian analysis would suggest that Holden fantasises about his own death to combat his fear of disappearing. Contrary to those critics who have read Holden as deeply affected by the loss of his brother, Mellard argues that 'it is less Allie's disappearance than his own that concerns Holden'.[137]

Mellard offers an interesting interpretation of the significance of Allie's mitt: obviously, the mitt signifies Allie (because it belonged to him), but it is also linked to Holden and his response to Allie's death. Allie was left-handed, so his mitt went on his right hand; Holden broke his right hand on the garage windows when Allie died and it has never completely healed. Mellard suggests that Holden's hand 'becomes identified with the loss of the brother, and so becomes related to the lost object of mourning'.[138] Indeed, his hand stopped Holden from completing his mourning for Allie: he missed his brother's funeral because he was in hospital receiving treatment for his injury. The link between Allie and Holden is also symbolised in Holden's red hat, which is an echo of Allie's red hair.[139]

Indeed, Holden's hat represents a new identity for him and it is significant that he regains the hat when he is reconciled with Phoebe, because his responsible reaction to her desire to run away with him shows that he now feels able to 'speak from the place of the father'; that is, he has attained 'fully mature subjectivity'.[140] Mellard contends that Holden's joy at this moment – as he watches Phoebe on the carrousel – suggests that, although he seems to tell his story from an institution in California, 'he no longer has any real need of therapy'.[141]

In their Marxist reading of the novel (see Critical history, **pp. 51–3**), the Ohmanns make it clear that they objected to the tendency of critics to assume that Holden is less an individual going through a personal crisis in a specific time and place, and more a universal representative of typical adolescent experience. Convincing as the Ohmanns are, few other critics acknowledge the very particular nature of Holden, and there has been a tendency to suggest that his experiences would be just the same if he were black or poor or female. In 1990, Mary Schriber published an essay that challenges the typical critical assumption that Holden is a universally recognisable figure. Schriber notes the immense popularity of *Catcher* and the substantial number of academic essays that have followed in its wake: 'Holden Caulfield has been constructed as a classic American hero, the American

135 Mellard, in Salzberg, *Critical Essays*, p. 201.
136 Mellard, in Salzberg, *Critical Essays*, p. 202.
137 Mellard, in Salzberg, *Critical Essays*, p. 203.
138 Mellard, in Salzberg, *Critical Essays*, p. 205.
139 Mellard, in Salzberg, *Critical Essays*, p. 206.
140 Mellard, in Salzberg, *Critical Essays*, pp. 210, 211.
141 Mellard, in Salzberg, *Critical Essays*, p. 211.

adolescent, and the whole of American youth.'[142] However, as Schriber comments, Holden is 'but a sixteen-year-old urban, male, WASP [White Anglo-Saxon Protestant] preppy': how is it that he has become a universal figure?[143]

Like George Steiner (see Critical history, p. 48), Schriber believes that *Catcher* criticism was initially driven by the surge in academic publishing that began in the late 1950s; unlike Steiner, though, she recognises that the criticism produced in this period was almost all written by men and that the novel was critiqued according to male values. This situation, along with the text's adolescent audience and the cult that arose around Salinger as a recluse has guaranteed *Catcher* continued attention that novels like Carson McCullers' *A Member of the Wedding* (1946) and Ella Leffland's *Rumors of Peace* (1979) have not received, probably because they are concerned with female adolescence, a subject less likely to interest male critics. Schriber asserts that, ultimately, the key to *Catcher*'s success is identification by critics with Holden: 'Falling in love with him as with their very selves, they fall in love with the novel as well. [. . .] they see in Holden [. . .] an incarnation of their youth.'[144] Schriber notes that various critics do declare their identification with Holden: they see themselves in him in their youth and in their adulthood. Back in 1951 when Ernest Jones contended that *Catcher* offers 'a case history of all of us', Schriber comments, he 'apparently defin[ed] "us" as male'.[145] Later, Brian Way's reading (see Critical history, pp. 46–7) of sexuality as central to the novel was comfortable with the assumption that Holden's sexual anxieties are 'universally adolescent', as if male and female sexuality are the same (or perhaps that only males are adolescent).[146]

When critics identify (or impose) the patterns of traditional literature – quest, dream, romance, rebellion – as critics of *Catcher* have often done, they are pursuing lines of enquiry that are 'unmistakeably masculinist, ratifying the identification of the reader with that which is male and leading critics to normalize, universalize, and canonize Holden Caulfield'.[147] To Schriber, *Catcher*'s critics are responsible for giving global significance to a character who is no more or less than 'a WASP preppy male youth'.[148] This act of making the specific into the universal means that terms like 'youth' and 'adolescence' become immasculated: terms that theoretically apply equally to men and women come to denote masculinity only. Schriber contends that 'androcentric' (that is, male-dominated) culture immasculates readers so that all readers, female and male, are 'duped into finding ourselves in Salinger's novel'.[149] She concludes that, whatever the strengths of the novel itself, criticism of *Catcher* is 'oblivious to the possibility of female perspective; it fails to problematize the male (and the urban and the WASP); it remains shackled to false and damaging universals'.[150] Schriber's essay is very unusual in its understanding of the novel and its critics, and she makes

---

142 Mary Suzanne Schriber, 'Holden Caulfield, C'est Moi', in Salzberg, *Critical Essays*, p. 226.
143 Schriber, in Salzberg, *Critical Essays*, p. 227.
144 Schriber, in Salzberg, *Critical Essays*, p. 227.
145 Schriber, in Salzberg, *Critical Essays*, p. 228.
146 Schriber, in Salzberg, *Critical Essays*, p. 228.
147 Schriber, in Salzberg, *Critical Essays*, p. 232.
148 Schriber, in Salzberg, *Critical Essays*, p. 233.
149 Schriber, in Salzberg, *Critical Essays*, p. 236.
150 Schriber, in Salzberg, *Critical Essays*, p. 236.

a very strong case that the unquestioned assumptions of critics have created a consensus about the novel's meaning, assuming that because they see themselves in the novel, so will everyone else. While there is no implication that Schriber considers every critical observation made about *Catcher* to be nonsense – plainly, there have been some very interesting essays which illuminate the text considerably – her central argument is very clear: 'an adolescent male WASP is not automatically nature's designated spokesperson for us all'.[151]

An interesting critical development in recent years has been interpretations of *Catcher* that consider it in relation to the Cold War. Alan Nadel's study of 'containment culture' (the repression that characterised American society in the 1950s described in Texts and contexts, **pp. 10–15**) includes a chapter on Holden Caulfield. Nadel suggests that Holden 'voices many of the domestic themes of containment and also demonstrates the impossibility of articulating those themes while speaking veracious [truthful] speech'.[152] So Nadel's reading of *Catcher* focuses on the ways in which Holden's speech and images in the novel invoke aspects of Cold War society. For example, Holden tells Ackley in Chapter 3 that his red cap is a 'people shooting hat': Nadel argues that this red hunting hat can be understood to be a hat worn for hunting 'reds' (Communists) which makes Holden a McCarthy-style pursuer of subversives. Indeed, Holden's constant disparagement of 'phonies' might imply that he is seeking truth and rejecting liars. However, Holden's narrative is also characterised by his tendency to 'name names', much as one of McCarthy's victims would be required to do, and Nadel notes the extraordinary number of names (of people and places) that Holden mentions as he tells his story.[153]

Nadel is aware of existing criticism of *Catcher* and comments on those early essays that compare the novel to *Huckleberry Finn*; Nadel contends that, unlike Huck, Holden has nowhere to run to, 'no river on which to flee, no western territory for which to light out', because for Holden 'the territory is mental, not physical'.[154] So for Holden the struggle is not, as it is for Huck, to find a place where he can be free, but to find a mental space in which he can think freely. Holden lives in a much more rule-governed society than Huck, argues Nadel, and this awareness is expressed even at the structural level of his narrative, through a pattern of 'specific example → generalisation → rule'. A typical example appears in the first chapter of the novel when Holden comments, 'somebody'd stolen my camel's-hair coat right out of my room [. . .] Pencey was full of crooks [. . .] The more expensive a school is, the more crooks it has' (Ch. 1, p. 3). In this sequence of comments, Holden begins with a specific example, follows with a generalisation and from these builds a rule. This pattern, says Nadel, suggests that: 'Caulfield not only explains his world but also justifies his explanations by locating them in the context of governing rules, rendering his speech not only compulsively explanatory but also authoritarian in that it must demonstrate an authority for *all*

151 Schriber, in Salzberg, *Critical Essays*, p. 236.
152 Alan Nadel, 'Rhetoric, Sanity, and the Cold War: The Significance of Holden Caulfield's Testimony', in Alan Nadel (ed.), *Containment Culture: American Narratives, Postmodernism and the Atomic Age*, Durham, NC and London: Duke University Press, 1995, p. 71.
153 Nadel, *Containment Culture*, p. 76.
154 Nadel, *Containment Culture*, p. 71.

his statements.'[155] Holden is constantly using his observations to develop theories and rules about himself and his society, suggesting that he is aware of the ways in which his society is characterised by issues of control. Holden can empower himself by seeming to create and apply his own rules, but to a great extent he is simply repressing his own individuality by applying such rules to himself.

Nadel is also aware of the work by Carol and Richard Ohmann (see Critical history, **pp. 51–3**), who read *Catcher* as a critique of the impact of capitalism. Nadel agrees that '*Catcher* may indeed be a vivid manifestation of the period's political unconscious' but plainly for this critic the focus of that political consciousness is on issues of repression rather than capitalism (although there is a link between the two).[156] Holden presents himself as a person who, in a phony era, is willing to tell the truth and expose the phony; indeed, comments Nadel, Holden's speech 'asserts its own veracity more than once for every page of narrative' through phrases such as 'I really did', 'I'm not kidding' and 'if you want to know the truth'.[157] Holden keeps telling the reader that he is a 'terrific liar', but uses a range of words and phrases to assure us that he is not a phony. Nadel believes that this aspect of the narrative affirms that it is a text produced in the context of a 'society plagued by loyalty oaths'.[158] Ultimately, however, swearing that a statement is true does not guarantee that it is: it simply shows that the speaker wishes to be believed.

Like John Howell (see Text and contexts, **pp. 47–8**), Nadel sees a link between the issues raised by *Catcher* and themes in the work of T. S. Eliot, especially in *The Waste Land*, in the sense that loss, alienation, failed relationships and a search for truth and faith are evident in both novel and poem. Nadel notes that *Catcher* shares these concerns with other texts of the period, partly because the trauma and repressions of the post-war/Cold War era encouraged such preoccupations and partly because the texts of 'high modernism' (of which *The Waste Land* is a key example) were still viewed as the epitome of serious literature in this period and were therefore worthy of emulation. As when earlier critics linked *Catcher* to a classic text, Nadel's comparison of the novel with Eliot's work affirms *Catcher*'s seriousness and literary value. Nadel's work – on *Catcher* specifically and on the 1950s in general – is interesting and convincing; his reading of Holden's narrative in terms of testimony is particularly stimulating.

Leerom Medovoi's 1997 essay on *Catcher* and the Cold War took account of Nadel's reading and aimed to develop the connection between the novel and its political context by arguing that during the Cold War, 'youth' came to symbolise 'American democratic character'.[159] The 1950s has been understood in a range of ways: as a 'golden' age; as a time of affluence and political consensus; as an age defined by fear of the foreign; as a period of racial inequality and repressive gender roles. Medovoi contends that the 1950s also saw the early stages of gay culture, civil rights activities, the Nation of Islam, the rise of counter-culture,

---

155 Nadel, *Containment Culture*, p. 72.
156 Nadel, *Containment Culture*, p. 74.
157 Nadel, *Containment Culture*, p. 76.
158 Nadel, *Containment Culture*, p. 72.
159 Leerom Medovoi, 'Democracy, Capitalism, and American Literature: The Cold War Construction of J. D. Salinger's Paperback Hero', in Joel Foreman (ed.), *The Other Fifties: Interrogating Midcentury American Icons*, Urbana, Ill.: University of Illinois Press, 1997, p. 257.

drugs and the Beats, youth culture and rock 'n' roll, all of which suggest that the era was not entirely conservative or repressed. In particular, Medovoi recognises that the era is seen as being especially hostile to its new youth culture but argues that, although delinquency may have been feared, the autonomy of youth was 'accepted as part of the cold war agenda'.[160] Many critics read *Catcher* as an 'insight into America's presumed youthful personality'; for example, Heiserman and Miller (see Critical history, **pp. 41–2**) link Holden to Huck Finn and praise Salinger's hero for rejecting the corruptions of adulthood.[161] This and other essays in the same vein seem to affirm the importance of non-conformity in young people as if non-conformity itself were an American ideal, a conclusion that does not suggest support for the repressions of the Cold War era. This reading of Holden highlights the ambivalence of the 1950s that, as Medovoi confirms, is a period that is difficult to define: if it were really the oppressive era it is often understood to be, no one would dare to praise a character in a best-selling novel who is both young and non-conformist.

The 1950s is also known as a period of economic expansion that relied on the success of capitalist values and was anti-Communist in practice and in ethos (see Texts and contexts, **pp. 9–13**). Medovoi notes the Ohmanns' assertion that the novel is anti-capitalist in its critique of class inequality (see Critical history, **pp. 51–3**); he contends that critics avoided a class-based reading of the novel in the 1950s and 1960s because of the pressures of anti-Communism. Instead, critics addressed generational difference, interpreting the novel as a psychological narrative of growing up. However, youth has a symbolic meaning in America: the USA considers itself to be a 'young' nation and so youth is a 'metaphor for America itself'.[162] Youth culture is in turn linked to capitalism, through consumerism. In the 1950s, capitalism was also strongly associated with democracy, not because capitalism is democratic but because correlating democracy with capitalism was politically useful: it encouraged its opposites, totalitarianism and communism, to be established as a comparable pair in the public mind. Although communism and totalitarianism are no more paired terms than democracy and capitalism, the implied connection encouraged the anti-Communism which fuelled political unity in the USA in the 1950s. So, oddly, youth culture in the period was simultaneously associated with non-conformity (and even be praised for it) and with capitalism (which was the epitome of conformist American society). Thus, despite the anxieties of some about the dangers of *Catcher* as a subversive novel and Holden as a delinquent, he could be read at the same time as the embodiment of key American values, a rebel with a moral core who could be seen as a role model. Holden Caulfield, teenage rebel, identifies what is phony in a range of social situations and in examples of low- and high-brow culture; he criticises people who place themselves on sale, whether for sex like Sunny or for acclaim like Ernie. One irony in this contradictory situation is that Holden himself, in the form of Salinger's novel, rapidly became a commodified part of 1950s youth culture and Salinger became an unwilling star who found himself on sale.

The contradictions that surround *Catcher* is a theme taken up by social historian

---

160 Medovoi, in Foreman, *The Other Fifties*, p. 257.
161 Medovoi, in Foreman, *The Other Fifties*, p. 260.
162 Medovoi, in Foreman, *The Other Fifties*, p. 259.

Pamela Hunt Steinle, who is especially interested in why the novel is so frequently banned in the USA. Although the novel does contain expletives, it is clear that Holden associates 'bad' language with corruption and is distressed by the negative impact of 'fuck you' on children, indicting the phrase as evidence of a flawed society. Holden could be read as anti-authoritarian in his critique of adult values but, for Steinle, that does not explain why the novel remains so controversial. She contends that hostility towards the text is 'indicative of a deepening cultural crisis in post-World War II America: a conflict or at the very least a lack of clarity as to what is believed about American adolescents'.[163]

Further, Steinle contends that negative responses to *Catcher* could be linked to what is perceived to be a widening gap between American ideals and the actual behaviour of Americans as individuals and of the USA as a nation. Debates about *Catcher* are provoked by – but also encourage – public expression of opinions that might otherwise stay private: opinions about social expectations of young people, ideas of Americanness, about morality and about literature. As Steinle says: 'Arguing ostensibly about whether or not *Catcher* is an appropriate reading for adolescents, participants often find themselves engaged in a gut-wrenching controversy over the definition and viability of our national character.'[164] Those debating its suitability as a text for young people may in fact be debating whether or not America has failed to live up to expectations. *Catcher* is not the only novel to raise doubts about American character – in individual or national terms – but it may be especially vulnerable to controversy because it is, as Steinle argues, more than a novel: it is a 'cultural statement', a text that can be claimed by any generation, that echoes through many other texts; a novel that can even change its reader.[165] As such, then, it is potentially dangerous and because it provokes anxieties the novel becomes the victim of censorship in a country that claims freedom of thought and action as founding values.

After more than fifty years of commentary on *The Catcher in the Rye*, critics are still finding provocative and engaging things to say about it. This chapter has discussed some of the most outstanding essays that have been written since the novel was published in 1951. The wide range of critical approaches and the steady stream of fresh readings suggest that stimulating interpretations of the novel will continue to appear well into the new century. Indeed, the next chapter (see Critical readings, **pp. 67–118**) offers five new essays commissioned for this study that all present challenging and innovative readings of the novel.

---

163 Pamela Hunt Steinle, *In Cold Fear: The Catcher in the Rye Censorship Controversies and Postwar American Character*, Columbus, Ohio: Ohio State University Press, 2000, p. 3.
164 Steinle, *In Cold Fear*, p. 3.
165 Steinle, *In Cold Fear*, p. 41.

3

Critical readings

Sally Robinson, 'Masculine protest in *The Catcher in the Rye*'

Sally Robinson is Associate Professor of English at Texas A&M University. Her most recent book is *Marked Men: White Masculinity in Crisis* (2000). She has also written articles on feminist theory, the teaching of masculinity studies, contemporary American fiction and film and is currently working on a book about masculinity and anti-consumerism in post-Second World War American culture. Like Leerom Medovoi and Alan Nadel, whose work is discussed in the Critical history (**pp. 63–5**), Robinson is particularly interested in the culture of 1950s America, especially in relation to masculinity studies. This area of gender studies challenges the idea that masculinity is 'natural' and tied to biological sex, focusing instead on the ways in which masculinity is 'socially constructed'. This means that masculinity is not inherent in a person born male, nor a fixed and definable characteristic, but is achieved through the performance of a complex act that imitates whatever is considered to be the masculine ideal in the society of a given place and time. A significant part of the power associated with masculinity derives from the assumption of its naturalness and unchanging qualities but, in fact, what is deemed to be masculine differs across history, geography and culture. Further, any individual's gender performance (whether masculine or feminine) can never be said to be fixed or stable: developed from and in response to a range of shifting social factors, gender is never simply possessed by an individual but is always in a state of construction and reconstruction. Robinson is interested in how masculinity was defined in post-war America: what social factors shaped its definition, what pressures were felt by those who were (unconsciously) engaged in the performance of masculinity at this time, and what was at stake for anyone who rejected conventional masculinity. In this essay, Robinson discusses the social studies that were popular in the 1950s (see Texts and contexts, **pp. 14–16**) and their contention that changes in American society had a negative impact on traditional masculinity, which was associated with individualism, freethinking and taking an active role. The boom in consumerism and the rise of corporate business meant that a successful man might now be one who relinquished his individuality and power, submitted himself to the rule of the group and accepted anonymity and conformity, all of which are antithetical to the traditions of American masculinity which were previously associated with America's success as a nation. Holden Caulfield poses a challenge to this model because he disparages conformity as 'phony' and demands the right to be himself, even if that means rejecting his own society.

Sally Robinson, 'Masculine protest in *The Catcher in the Rye*'

The Catcher in the Rye was published in an era that produced a large body of social criticism read by a mass audience as well as an academic one. Books like William Whyte's *The Organization Man* (1957), C. Wright Mills's *White Collar* (1951), and David Riesman's *The Lonely Crowd* (1953) set the terms for public debate about post-war changes in economic, political and social systems. These books have had an influence on American culture that is hard to overestimate: 'the Organization Man,' like 'the Man in the Gray Flannel Suit,' became a cultural icon that, more than fifty years later, still appears in the pages of business and news magazines. These books tapped into a vein of cultural anxiety about what was to become of the individual in a future structured by bureaucracies and corporate 'groupthink' (in which it is more important to agree than to develop good ideas). Authenticity appeared to be under threat in a consumer culture organised not only around buying but also the necessity of selling oneself. In turn, Whyte, Mills, Riesman and others helped to shape the discourse about the social effects of widespread economic changes. These texts do not couch their social criticism in gender terms, but they do, nevertheless, have a great deal to say about how the changing economic and social terrain affects American masculinity. Indeed, read against books like Philip Wylie's attack on female dominance of the domestic and sexual realms (dubbed 'Momism') in *A Generation of Vipers* (1942), and articles like Arthur Schlesinger's 'The Crisis of Masculinity' (1958), it seems clear that gender concerns were never far below the surface of texts which seem to have nothing, overtly, to say about gender. All of these texts, and countless magazine articles, detail a broad 'feminization' of white, middle-class American men. Taken together, they articulate a form of masculine protest against the increasingly strong and pervasive dominance of consumerism (attachment to material goods) in American life. Consumerism was long thought to threaten masculinity because it instilled false feminine values in place of authentic male virtues, and it replaced autonomy with dependence on market forces. A wide range of new business and organisational practices – including rising bureaucratisation (increasingly complex administrative procedures), the popularity and influence of market research, and the new 'sciences' of management and personality testing – threaten to displace older understandings of American masculine power and self-reliance, rendering the once active male producer of earlier eras into the passive consumer of the 1950s. It is in this context that I will place *The Catcher in the Rye*, reading Holden's rebellion as part of a larger tradition of masculine protest rather than as an adolescent protest unmodified by gender.

The overarching thematic of the social critics writing at mid-century concerns fears that large social structures – the corporation, the bureaucracy, consumerism

– aim to control the individual by forcing him to submit his initiative to their power, rendering him passive, weak, and feminised. Whyte, Mills and Riesman offered ambitious and totalising theories to trace the source of changes in American character and to detail their social and psychological effects. Riesman's analysis is most explicitly concerned with defining an emerging 'American character', but Wright, Whyte and Salinger also engage in a form of protest against what they present as an identifiable shift in national identity. Terms like 'consensus' and 'conformity', widely circulated within both popular and academic sociology in the period, point to a shared suspicion that what made America great – in the colonial and frontier eras – is endangered by a set of institutions that all conspire to deprive the American (man) of his autonomy and authenticity. *The Catcher in the Rye* adds the term 'phoniness' to this lexicon of crisis. While most critics of *Catcher* connect 'phoniness' with the compromises required of adulthood, this view ignores the evidence of far more widespread anxiety over the threats to authenticity in the post-war era. Holden becomes a spokesperson, not for adolescent discontent or rebellion, but for a form of masculine protest that was itself fast becoming part of the post-war consensus.

Some critics of *Catcher* have already pointed to the novel's relationship to contemporaneous sociological discourses concerned with diagnosing the condition of the 'American character' at mid-century (Seelye, Brookeman, and Steinle, for example).[1] However, the relevance of these discourses to the novel's engagement with gender has escaped notice. Neither *Catcher* nor the sociological critique has been read as having *anything* to say about gender because none of these texts has much to say about women. In Whyte's *The Organization Man*, for example, women are featured only as the wives of organisation men, and Wright Mills in *White Collar* conflates the middle-class person with the middle-class man. More interesting, however, than the expected exclusion of women's concerns from the sociological analysis is the way in which these studies rely on the language of gender to make their case that the American character is in decline; while *women* might be absent from these pages, fear of *femininity* is everywhere evident. As Robert Corber notes, Mills diagnoses the decline of self-made manhood as a 'feminization of male subjectivity'.[2] Whyte's *The Organization Man*, in many ways, encapsulates the historical moment as a crisis in masculinity. The book is an impassioned plea for a return to competitive individualism, and, although Whyte never identifies competitive individualism with masculinity, he couches his critique in terms that invoke an opposition between a strong America characterised by self-made manhood and rugged individualism and a weak America characterised by the individual's subordination to a social system. When Whyte summarises the organisation man's condition as one of overwhelming passivity, his use of the generic 'people' to mask the specific 'men' fails to disguise the gendered dynamic at work here: 'Once people liked to think, at least, that they were in control of their destinies, but few of the younger organization people

---

1 John Seelye and Christopher Brookeman in Jack Salzman (ed.), *New Essays on The Catcher in the Rye*, Cambridge: Cambridge University Press, 1991. Pamela Hunt Steinle, *In Cold Fear: The Catcher in the Rye Censorship Controversies and Postwar American Character*, Columbus, Ohio: Ohio State University Press, 2000.
2 Robert Corber, *Homosexuality in Cold War America: Resistance and the Crisis of Masculinity*, Durham, NC and London: Duke University Press, 1997, p. 33.

cherish such notions. Most see themselves as objects more acted upon than acting – and their future, therefore, determined as much by the system as by themselves.'[3]

Running through all of these books, and countless magazine articles from the period, is the suspicion that gender difference is eroding as men begin to look, act, and behave more like women are supposed to, and women start to benefit from their symbolic power as the embodiment of a consumer ethos. For Whyte, American men have become merely numbers in a bureaucratic equation. In Riesman's account, the 'other-directed' man produced by the shift from a production to a consumption economy has no core self or character in the tradition of American individualism; he 'tends to become merely his succession of roles and encounters and hence to doubt who he is or what he is'.[4] Mills most directly invokes the core anxiety provoked by the spread of consumerism when he notes that the white-collar workers 'sell not only their time and energy but their personalities as well'.[5] While women might, in fact, be accustomed to having to sell themselves, this is a new experience for men and, according to these critics, one that has dire consequences for the future of American masculinity. Like Riesman, Whyte and Mills, Salinger's protagonist bemoans the 'prostitutions' required for full male membership in American culture. As Leerom Medovoi notes, 'phoniness' in *Catcher* is not limited to those who enjoy class privilege, as some readings of the novel suggest; instead, the term is applicable to any individual who produces himself as a commodity to be sold. Phonies are those 'whose self-promotion for the consumption of others is an index of their inauthenticity'.[6] While Holden deems women, as well as men, to be 'phonies', phoniness in women is more or less expected, with their 'damn falsies that point all over the place' and their devotion to fashion and celebrities (Ch. 1, p. 2).

Significantly, it is the writer, the teacher, and others who make their living by words who most often provoke Holden's rage at phoniness. D. B., we're told at the outset, is 'out in Hollywood [. . .] being a prostitute' (Ch. 1, p. 1), while Holden's father is a corporate lawyer who finances Broadway shows. Advertisers and others who twist words to manipulate reality are the targets of Holden's contempt. The subjection of the writer to the demands of the marketplace has historically been cause for concern in American culture. As amply demonstrated in a wide range of cultural and literary histories, American writers, particularly male writers, have long positioned themselves as heroic individuals seeking to tell the truth in a commercial culture where the values of celebrity and popularity trump the values of authenticity and originality. As Paul Gilmore argues convincingly in the aptly titled *The Genuine Article*, the great American writers of the late nineteenth and early twentieth century felt themselves to be fighting against the corruptions of the feminine marketplace. Being a

3   William Whyte, *The Organization Man*, Garden City, NY: Doubleday Anchor Books, 1957, p. 437.
4   David Riesman, *The Lonely Crowd: A Study of the Changing American Character*, New Haven, Conn.: Yale University Press, 1969, p. 139.
5   C. Wright Mills, *White Collar: The American Middle Classes*, Oxford: Oxford University Press, 2002, p. xvii.
6   Medovoi, in Foreman, *The Other Fifties*, p. 277.

manly writer meant resisting commercial demands. Because their profession and the literary market were largely imagined in feminine terms and because many of the most successful authors were women, male authors often oscillated between a desire for commercial success and a need to define themselves as independent creators resistant to a feminizing marketplace.[7]

The figure of the prostitute most often illustrates this anxiety over commercialisation as feminisation.

Against D. B.'s prostituted talent, Salinger positions two forms of anti-commercial and, thus, authentic writing: the writing on Allie's baseball glove and Phoebe's novels featuring Hazel Weatherby. Much has been made of the novel's privileging of these two youthful Caulfield siblings as the figures of the childhood innocence that Holden desperately aims to hold on to, but their significance as representatives of an anti-commercial, anti-consumerist ethos is equally important. In Holden's imagination, Allie and Phoebe occupy an innocent, non-consumer paradise uncorrupted by those 'phonies' who allow the movies, advertising, and corporate values to define and commodify their identities. Interestingly, these two characters are also free from the gender conventions that Holden struggles with, because they are both represented as androgynous (not being strongly identified as male or female). Allie and Phoebe represent not only Holden's lost childhood, but also a lost social and cultural order where authenticity has not yet given way to phoniness. Outside the conventions of gender, Allie and Phoebe are not subject to the 'feminisation' that Holden fears or the 'masculinisation' he ambivalently accepts. Masculinisation, in this context, means acceptance of mass-produced norms of mature manhood, modelled by Holden's corporate attorney father and the various businessmen who govern the prep schools he has attended. Ironically, this masculinisation also means feminisation: mindless adaptation to a social order that denies the individual (man) power to determine his own fate.

Holden's fears of becoming just another Organisation Man (like his father) and of getting sucked into consumer culture (like D. B.) are balanced against fears of what it would mean to opt out of successful masculinity as it is currently defined. As Barbara Ehrenreich and others have argued, men who chose not to pursue the dream of domestic masculinity in the 1950s were often suspected to be homosexual.[8] Holden is certainly subject to worries about sexual orientation, seeing 'flits' around every corner and pondering the warning of his old mentor, Carl Luce:

> He said half of the married guys in the world were flits and didn't even know it. He said you could turn into one practically overnight, if you had all the traits and all. He used to scare the hell out of us. I kept waiting to turn into a flit or something. The funny thing about old Luce, I used to think he was sort of flitty himself.
>
> (Ch. 19, p. 129)

7   Paul Gilmore, *The Genuine Article: Race, Mass Culture, and American Literary Manhood*, Durham, NC and London: Duke University Press, 2001, p. 13.
8   Barbara Ehrenreich, *The Hearts of Men: American Dreams and the Flight from Commitment*, New York: Anchor Books, 1983.

Holden's ambivalence about aligning himself with 'mature masculinity' is most clearly demonstrated in that odd scene in which he proposes to Sally Hayes that they escape into the woods. Sally, speaking for responsibility, domesticity, and materialism, unsurprisingly rejects Holden's fantasy. As Holden quickly understands, Sally represents the road to the very thing he yearns to escape from 'working in some office, making a lot of dough, and riding to work in cabs and Madison Avenue buses, and reading newspapers, and playing bridge all the time, and going to the movies and seeing a lot of stupid shorts and coming attractions and newsreels' (Ch. 17, pp. 119–20). Given Holden's resistance to the very idea of domesticity and breadwinning, his response to Sally makes perfect sense; what doesn't make sense is his confession, earlier, that 'I felt like marrying her the minute I saw her. I'm crazy. I didn't even *like* her much, and yet all of a sudden I felt like I was in love with her and wanted to marry her' (Ch. 17, p. 112). Holden doesn't actually 'feel' in love with Sally: he is seduced by both a mass-produced version of heterosexual romance and mature masculinity – and resents that seduction. His ambivalence about gender is further evidenced by the fact that he habitually performs a Hollywood-produced masculinity (in Chapter 14, for example, when he copes with Maurice's attack by pretending to be shot) while voicing a violent opposition to Hollywood.

Holden's extreme emotional investment in depicting mass culture as endangering the values of originality, creativity and authenticity connects Salinger's novel to a more general mass-culture critique being mounted by mid-century intellectuals. Dwight MacDonald's famous *Partisan Review* essay 'Masscult and Midcult' (1960) reads as a supplement to Holden Caulfield's condemnation of the 'phony' culture he finds everywhere around him. Each example of 'phoniness' in the novel relates to a performer's effort to please an audience rather than to express a personal belief, aesthetic or truth. Speeches made at the various prep schools Holden attends, movies and shows, Ernie's piano-playing: each performance is corrupted by the performer pandering to the audience's desires and expectations. Responding to Ernie's artistic compromises, Holden swears allegiance to an ethic of creative genius, in which the artist retains his integrity only by maintaining his independence from an audience: '[I]f I were a piano player or an actor or something and all those dopes thought I was terrific, I'd hate it. I wouldn't even want them to *clap* for me. People always clap for the wrong things. If I were a piano player, I'd play it in the goddam closet' (Ch. 12, pp. 76–7). For MacDonald, there is no doubt that the problem with 'masscult' (culture modified for presentation through mass media) is that 'mere popularity' determines merit in the marketplace of consumer culture. Popularity is not the problem per se, for MacDonald notes that some high cultural texts have been popular; the problem is that, in masscult, we find 'impersonality,' 'lack of standards,' and 'total subjection to the spectator'.[9] 'Today, in the United States,' he writes, 'the demands of the audience, which has changed from a small body of connoisseurs into a large body of ignoramuses, have become the chief criteria of success.'[10] While neither Salinger nor MacDonald employs an overtly gendered rhetoric to critique mass

9 Dwight MacDonald, 'Masscult and Midcult', *Partisan Review*, 1960, reprinted in D. MacDonald, *Against the American Grain*, New York: Da Capo Press, 1962, p. 7.
10 MacDonald, *Against the American Grain*, p. 18.

culture, gender nevertheless is implicit in these laments for the lost days of solitary genius and independence of mind. Code words for 'feminine' culture abound in MacDonald's critique, in which 'the cheapest, flimsiest kind of melodrama', 'bathetic sentimentality', and 'the most vulgar kind of theatricality' compete with 'the most acute psychological analysis and social observation', 'superb comedy', and 'great descriptive prose'.[11] Melodrama, sentimentality, and theatricality are linked with the feminine in an aesthetic system that, as Andreas Huyssen and others have argued, ties true creativity to the masculine. The modern male artist, 'the suffering loner who stands in irreconcilable opposition to modern democracy and its inauthentic culture', must battle against the 'phoniness' which defines mass culture and distances it from the authentic, masculine expression of true artistic genius.[12]

The pull of this romantic ideology is so strong that it appears even where we might least expect to find it: in William Whyte's analysis of the rise of the Organisation Man in the business world. Like MacDonald, who claims that a 'mass society, like a crowd, is inchoate [indistinct] and uncreative', Whyte criticises the new social ethic for destroying the possibility and power of individual genius.[13] The 'false collectivisation' driving the new emphasis on creative groups, rather than creative individuals, is based on a mistaken belief that groups 'think' and 'create'. Whyte argues that group advocates, who are now dominant in the sciences and humanities, 'are engaged in a wholesale effort to tame the arts of discovery – and those by nature suited for it. In part this effort is propelled by the natural distaste of the uncreative man for the creative', but it is also part of the self-justifying strategy through which the individual must necessarily be subordinated to the group.[14] The solitary genius – the artist writing in his isolated garret, the scientist alone in his lab – is endangered by the collectivisation of creativity. As Whyte would have it, the decline of an ideology of competitive individualism in 'The Fight Against Genius' means the death of creativity itself.[15]

While Whyte does not explicitly address the effect of large organisations and bureaucracies on literature and the other arts, Janice Radway's work on the Book-of-the-Month Club makes it clear that gender was a primary cause of concern for those cultural critics worrying over new forms of literary production, selection and distribution. Anxieties over book clubs usurping the authority of more traditional literary gatekeepers dovetail with more general anxieties over the effects of standardisation on American character, creativity and autonomy. Radway argues that the debates over the cultural effects of book clubs were 'underwritten by broader, more widespread fears about [. . .] the fate of individual agency in a world growing more bureaucratic and regimented at every turn'.[16] Further, a 'profound gender anxiety' would 'make itself felt within the literary field as a form of deep distaste for the purported feminization of culture and

11 MacDonald, *Against the American Grain*, p. 7.
12 Andreas Huyssen, 'Mass Culture as Woman' in T. Modleski (ed.), *Studies in Entertainment: Critical Approaches to Mass Culture*, Bloomington, Ind.: Indiana University Press, 1986, p. 194.
13 MacDonald, *Against the American Grain*, p. 9.
14 Whyte, *The Organization Man*, p. 57.
15 MacDonald, *Against the American Grain*, p. 225.
16 Janice Radway, *A Feeling for Books: The Book-of-the-Month Club, Literary Taste, and Middle-Class Desire*, Chapel Hill, NC: University of North Carolina Press, 1997, p. 189.

the emasculation of otherwise assertive artists and aggressively discriminating readers': writers and readers alike are threatened by the feminising forces of consumer culture.[17] MacDonald's worry that audiences are usurping the power of the creator is shared by Salinger, but the audience is also threatened with a feminisation, for the lack of discrimination and the confusion of standards robs the truly discerning reader – such as Holden Caulfield – of the power and authority to make authentic critical judgements. That *Catcher* was chosen as a Book-of-the-Month Club main selection – and that it was mass-marketed in paperback with a sensationalist cover – suggests that the mass-culture critique in the USA was so much a part of the popular discourse that it could, paradoxically, *itself* be commodified. Holden's rebellion against mass culture, like his rebellion against conformity, places him *not* in a select group of outsiders or rebels, but squarely within the dominant intellectual mode of his era. The masculine protest against feminisation articulated by Whyte, MacDonald and others is at mid-century a primary mode of identity-formation, in addition to being a primary mode for reproducing gender.

Like the post-war discourse engaged in diagnosing disturbing changes to 'the American character', *The Catcher in the Rye* hides its anxieties about gender difference beneath a narrative about conformity, consensus and phoniness. When speaking of 'American character' these social critics are in actuality speaking about a tradition of American masculinity based in an economy of production and on the naturalisation of a model of competitive individualism that cannot stand the stresses of new business models, new modes of consumption and new sciences to explain human desires and behaviours. Lizabeth Cohen notes that as the social critics of the 1950s were bemoaning the standardisation and mechanisation of a consumer culture that homogenises individuals into one mass, advertisers and others were already moving ahead to create what might turn out to be a greater threat to notions of masculine individualism, authenticity and autonomy.[18] Market segmentation – the strategy of identifying consumers by their race, class and gender – was to lead to a commodification of identity that Whyte and his fellow critics could only imagine.

The Catcher in the Rye seems to acknowledge that phoniness is here to stay, and this accounts for a good portion of its pleasurable tone of melancholy and nostalgia, a tone created by the novel's protest against an inevitable series of shifts and changes. Holden's lament is, as I have argued, part of a larger tradition of masculine protest: protest against threats to masculinity and protest as an expression, however compromised, of masculine power and authority. Such masculine protest against an always-rising tide of feminisation functions to reinforce gender difference even as it appears to be offering evidence of its destabilisation. *The Catcher in the Rye* might lack the social analysis of a book like *The Lonely Crowd*, but it articulates the same kind of masculine protest against changing economic and social conditions. That protest has the effect, not of creating *new* forms of masculinity, but of creating a nostalgic desire for the old forms, even as those forms become increasingly impossible to maintain.

17 Radway, *A Feeling for Books*, p. 189.
18 Lizabeth Cohen, *A Consumer's Republic: The Politics of Mass Consumption in Postwar America*, New York: Alfred A. Knopf, 2003.

Renée R. Curry, 'Holden Caulfield is not a person of colour'

Renée R. Curry, Professor of English, is Dean of the College of Arts, Humanities, and Social Sciences at California State University Monterey Bay. Her most recent article (forthcoming in *Sagetrieb*) addresses whiteness in the poetry of contemporary white women poets. Her most recent book is *White Women Writing White: H. D., Elizabeth Bishop, Sylvia Plath and Whiteness* (1999). She edited *Perspectives on Woody Allen* (1996) and co-edited *States of Rage: Violence, Emotional Eruption, and Social Change* (1996).
Curry is particularly interested in a relatively new field of research known as 'critical whiteness studies' which, amongst other things, challenges the unspoken convention that having a racial identity means being 'not white', as if whiteness were not itself a signifier of race. Because white is the dominant racial identity in the USA, it has become effectively invisible: it is the 'norm' against which any race not marked by whiteness is considered the 'other'. Invisibility means that white people's own racial identity is masked to them and so they are discouraged from recognising that their social standing may well derive in great part from their privileged status as white, rather than something unique to them as individuals. Critical whiteness studies is considered controversial by some commentators who see it as an attack on white people that blames them for exploiting other races and for being selfishly unaware of the advantages they enjoy, rather than celebrating the social contribution of white people (as African-American studies or women's studies, for example, might be expected to do for the sectors they explore). Whiteness studies range from politics and economics to assessing the impact of racial issues on culture. Literary criticism that is informed by critical whiteness studies might consider how the racial identities of the characters in a novel are represented and to what effect. Often, for example, characters are presumed to be white unless information is given to the contrary: this demonstrates the ways in which white racial identity is hidden and its status as the norm and ideal is affirmed. Curry's essay explores the representation of racial identity in Catcher, analysing both the ways in which people who are not white are represented and how Holden's identity as a white male – with all the privileges that implies – is established for the reader without direct statement. As well

as breaking new ground in considering the novel in terms of race, this essay also makes an important contribution to the argument, first voiced by the Ohmanns and pursued by Schriber (see Critical history, **pp. 61–3**), that Holden Caulfield is far from being a 'universal' figure who represents all adolescents, regardless of their race, culture, class or gender. Some introductory material on race relations in post-war America is included in Texts and contexts, **p. 13**.

Renée R. Curry, 'Holden Caulfield is not a person of colour'

The Catcher in the Rye and Holden Caulfield are often described as 'universal', implying that both the text and its protagonist express perfectly the alienation experienced by all adolescents as they come of age in the USA. The following description of Holden Caulfield's vast impact on our understanding of youth society is typical:

> With Holden, Salinger prefigured the juvenile delinquency of the 1950s, the 'drop-out' mentality of the 1960s generation, and the general disquiet among much of today's youth. With Holden, Salinger foresaw the generation gap that emerged in the 1960s and, to a certain extent, never disappeared. Holden has become, then, a lasting symbol of restless American youth.[1]

The idea that literature offers us 'universals', 'archetypes' and 'symbols' is an old one that has served readers well in their general understanding of literature. However, literary texts can also reveal 'particulars' experienced by 'specific' groups of people. A reading I propose of Holden Caulfield is one that asks us to read him through his 'particular' attributes: an upper-class, adolescent, white male who is coming of age in mid-twentieth-century New York. This reading suggests that Holden's story, while a significant and well-known one, is only one of many particular and individual stories, told and untold, about adolescents of all classes, races and genders who were also coming of age in the multifaceted New York at the same time as Holden. Such a reading might minimise the universality of Holden's particular experience, but it multiplies our awareness of all the stories that need to be situated next to his in order for us to appreciate the complex social fabric that constructed Holden and others during this period of time.

The fact that Holden is an upper-class white male is key to understanding him fully. Naming Holden's whiteness permits all audiences to grapple overtly with the white particularities of the text as well as the naïve and perhaps insidious ways in which audiences for fifty years have been able to generalise Holden's experience. Holden Caulfield is not a person of colour, yet when he is described as a 'symbol of American youth', we are permitted to presume he could represent any adolescent in the USA. However, he cannot represent people of colour because his life experience inside his white body is determined by factors such as class, race

---

1   Paul Alexander, *Salinger*, Los Angeles, Calif.: Renaissance Books, 1999, p. xv.

and gender. In the novel, we know Holden is not a person of colour because persons of colour in the text are labelled – 'Coloreds', 'Chinese', 'Indians' – while Holden's body is not labelled in this way. No language is used to describe his race, thus setting Holden apart as not-coloured, not Chinese and not Indian. Ironically, we know Holden is white because the novel never says he is white. Only other skin colours are named. Holden not only separates himself out racially by naming 'other' ethnic and racial groupings, but we also know he is a particular white young man because he separates himself out from other white privileged young men at his school, thus clarifying his sense of class distinctions.

But what exactly does it mean for a sixteen-year-old to understand himself as a white man unlike other white men? Literary critic Valerie Babb argues that American immigrants, unlike white affluent peoples born in America, understand their Americanness as something into which they have transformed. They report being 'made into Americans', and in this process, becoming enabled to attain 'freedom'. These immigrants define freedom as being able to access education, fulfil personal dreams, attain economic security and participate in democracy. Babb claims that: 'Within this broad definition are implicit assumptions, however, that the "real" American identity is a white, Protestant, and economically privileged one.'[2] Thus, by entering into a discussion of Holden Caulfield as a white man unlike other white men of the time, we participate in an integrated discussion of his race, assumptions, freedoms, class, education, economic security and place in society. Such integration is critical to conversations currently prevalent under the rubric of critical whiteness studies. Holden is not white simply by virtue of his skin colour: he is white by virtue of all the assumptions his whiteness permits him to make about his Americanness and his mobility in society. As Nobel Prize-winning author Toni Morrison reminds us: 'Deep within the word "American" is its association with race [. . .] American means white.'[3]

My discussion addresses not only the exceeding universality awarded to Holden's experiences, but also the need for all readers to understand that Holden's story is a story about a white boy. *The Catcher in the Rye* describes one adolescent experience, and we must know that a plurality of vastly different racialised experiences occurred in New York during the 1940s/1950s. As Carol and Richard Ohmann point out: 'Holden lives in a time and place, and these provide the material against which his particular adolescent sensibility reacts.'[4] Although the Ohmanns never address the whiteness of Holden's bourgeois life, they provide foundational insights regarding the importance of receiving a text and describing the power of a text in global contextual terms. These are the insights upon which I will expand.

Understanding Holden Caulfield as a particular white man who sees New York in a particularly white way requires that we define whiteness itself as an unfixed and plural category of social being. Woody Doane summarises a way to discern

---

2   Valerie Babb, *Whiteness Visible: The Meaning of Whiteness in American Literature*, New York: New York University Press, 1998, p. 121.
3   Toni Morrison, *Playing in the Dark: Whiteness and the American Literary Imagination*, New York: Knopf, 1992, p. 47.
4   Carol Ohmann and Richard Ohmann, 'Reviewers, Critics, and *The Catcher in the Rye*', in Salzberg, *Critical Essay*, p. 129.

this category: ' "Whiteness", like race, is a socially constructed category that reflects social relationships: *it cannot be understood apart from racialized social systems* [. . .] The essential point is that different – and even contradictory – forms of "whiteness" may coexist.'[5]

The fact that Holden even remotely understands himself and his circle of prep-school acquaintances as affluent, bourgeois and snobbish evidences Doane's point that not all white people understand whiteness similarly. Holden Caulfield is a rare white 1950s character in literature who can somewhat name himself, some of his privileges and other whites. Many discussions in critical whiteness studies have centred on the idea that whiteness, and its associated social privileges for upper-class white males, is often invisible to white people; however, in the case of Holden Caulfield, the often assumed invisibility of whiteness is not wholly true. He does vaguely 'see' his own whiteness and that of his peer group, but the more significant question is whether he understands his racialised position as one highly susceptible to white racism.

Just because Holden can indistinctly see himself as a white man does not mean that he understands his life as one embedded in a racialised social system, nor that he perceives himself to be part of the particularly privileged class of white males which maintains the racialised social system. The current conversations within critical whiteness studies point toward the dangers of further privileging white-ness by only noting how it is socially constructed and not critiquing its key role in the maintenance of white racism and inequitable social systems.[6] The purpose of this essay is not to privilege further the already privileged work of J. D. Salinger, *Catcher* and Holden Caulfield. Salinger's writing has already been reified as the 'most influential body of work in English prose by anyone since Hemingway' and *Catcher* as 'the indispensable manual from which cool styles of disaffection could be borrowed'.[7] Instead I concur with Stephen J. Whitfield who argues that: 'Holden remains confined to his era, unable to connect the dots from those cliques [that Holden renounces at Pencey Prep] to a larger society that might merit some rearrangement.'[8] My essay aligns with Whitfield's critique of the novel's apolitica-lity and passivity, but it also furthers the argument in terms of Holden's whiteness being the root cause of his naïveté and lack of knowledge about his surroundings.

I suggest that not only is Holden confined to his era, he is confined to perceive only a very small slice of his own era. And yet, Holden's nervous system, which will break down and cause him to be institutionalised by the end of the novel, senses that something is about to change or has already begun to change the core of his identity and being. Perhaps Holden's nervous system experiences, before his mind can comprehend, what Doane describes as the foundational recasting of white power in the USA that occurred in the 1950s:

> Beginning in the 1950s, the Civil Rights movement and related social
> movements succeeded in recasting the politics of race in the United

5   Ashley W. Doane, 'Rethinking Whiteness Studies', in Ashley W. Doane and Eduardo Bonilla-Silva (eds), *White Out: The Continuing Significance of Racism*, New York: Routledge, 2003, p. 7.

6   Doane, in Doane and Eduardo Bonilla-Silva, *White Out*, p. 17.

7   Stephen Whitfield, 'Cherished and Cursed: Toward a Social History of *The Catcher in the Rye*', *The New England Quarterly*, 70, 1997, p. 568.

8   Whitfield, 'Cherished and Cursed', p. 587.

States. Particularly significant in this process were challenges to white domination and exclusion [. . .] Implicit in this process was a challenge to the historical foundations of whiteness; that is, an attack on the legitimation of a white identity grounded in claims to white supremacy and the casting of whiteness as a positive and normalized alternative to a negatively defined racial 'other'.[9]

Figuratively, Holden Caulfield feels the earth shaking beneath his feet, and he seems to experience a hazy shifting in his white identity system. However, the changes make such subtle entry into Holden's world that he actually articulates no outward understanding of his racialised and class-based participation in the complex social system of post-Second World War New York. Rather, his nervous system simply breaks down by the end of the novel as he moves further and further away from his white school and affluent white male friends. Although he no longer desires to be associated with the elite white students of Pencey, after deciding to leave the school, Holden acknowledges in Chapter 1, 'I felt like I was sort of disappearing. It was that kind of a crazy afternoon, terrifically cold, and no sun out or anything, and you felt like you were disappearing every time you crossed a road' (Ch. 1, p. 4). Having decided to leave his white school and, figuratively speaking, having stepped away from a small part of his white self, he feels himself lacking in identity and being. Without a connection to whiteness, Holden does not feel present in his body; moreover, every time he 'crosses' over onto a new path, he experiences more sensations of disappearing. And yet, we come to understand that Holden cannot fully know nor move away from the whiteness within him.

By recognising and analysing Holden's lack of understanding of the whiteness that emanates from within him, we may begin to reread *Catcher* with an eye toward its racialised historical and social context. *Catcher* was published in July 1951, which embedded the text in the social, racial, and political landscape of post-Second World War New York. This time and place were profoundly transformational in terms of understandings of race. New York's 'African-American population rose from 150,000 in 1920, the era of the Harlem Renaissance, to nearly 750,000 by 1950, the first year of the decade that marked the struggle over civil rights'.[10] Real estate was racially distributed, which meant it was highly unlikely that people of different races would live in the same neighbourhoods. Thus, Holden has very little contact with African-American peoples or any other peoples of colour in the novel.

As a white person, Holden Caulfield is completely unknowledgeable about how people unlike him live. He walks where he chooses, he takes his chosen form of transportation, he frequents bars of his choosing and lives in select neighborhoods. He feels quite comfortable moving about the city, and even when he finds himself in a 'crumby hotel' on the Westside, his choice was intentional, and it permitted him some privacy from seeing the usual people of his Eastside society. Throughout all of his movements, he remains naïvely unaware that his comfort and his range of choice stems from his whiteness.

---

9 Doane, in Doane and Eduardo Bonilla-Silva, *White Out*, p. 15.
10 Shaun O'Connell, *Remarkable, Unspeakable New York: A Literary History*, Boston, Mass.: Beacon, 1995, p. 232.

The apartment in which Holden lives signifies his family's status as both upper middle class and white: the building has an elevator boy, there are only two apartments on each floor, and inside there is a maid's room, a bedroom for each child, and more. At first glance, Holden's New York living situation seems only marked by class; however, Johnson and Shapiro claim that such distinctions are also clearly marked by race.[11] J. D. Salinger designed the Caulfield's apartment in this way because he knew what it meant to live, as the Caulfields do, in a 'good' neighbourhood, a white neighbourhood distinctly not Harlem nor the bohemian Greenwich Village. Salinger's own family of origin moved him from northern Harlem just after Salinger was born in 1919. They moved to 113th Street, to West 82nd Street, and then to Park Avenue, all moves intentionally chosen by his father to 'elevate' the family to more affluent white neighbourhoods.[12] As Alexander claims, it is clear throughout the novel that Salinger is critical of the upwardly mobile lifestyles of the rich and that *Catcher* intentionally explores and critiques certain aspects of elite living. Simultaneously, however, Salinger explores little about and demonstrates minimal understanding of the white racial power embedded in the living arrangements of his main character.

Like Salinger, his family, and many other white peoples, Holden Caulfield assumes an individuality determined by choices. *Catcher's* opening lines deliver an attitude of petulant capitulation wielded by a white adolescent, Holden Caulfield: 'If you really want to hear about it, the first thing you'll probably want to know is where I was born, and what my lousy childhood was like, and how my parents were occupied and all before they had me' (Ch. 1, p. 1). The position that the reader is supposed to undertake, given this opening, is one of pleading with Holden to tell his uniquely interesting story. Readers of *Catcher* have been presumed to be people who would have sufficient knowledge of and empathy with predominately white, upper-middle-class adolescents with enough resources to roam New York City streets comfortably for a few days. If we read the opening pages of the text in this way, it becomes clear that the audience addressed by Holden is an extremely particular and narrow set of affluent white readers with experiences of the world dependent upon upper-class societal opportunities, not the universal and generalised set of readers presumed to be addressed by the text, namely almost all the high-school students in the USA to whom the book has often been assigned reading for the past fifty years.

Valerie Babb explores this type of white presumption which often occurs in cultural and literary texts. She writes that all too frequently a white presumptiveness remains invisible in literary texts, but it can be unwittingly marked in texts in which 'only white characters foster cultural perceptions'.[13] Holden Caulfield's observations are perfect examples of just such white fostering of cultural perceptions presumed to be generalisable and universal. His perceptions about adolescent alienation in the 1950s are actually quite particular to a small white set of people; many people would have markedly different perceptions of this time period in this same city.

---

11 Heather Beth Johnson and Thomas M. Shapiro, in Doane and Bonilla-Silva, *White Out*, p. 176.
12 Alexander, *Salinger*, pp. 33–5.
13 Babb, *Whiteness Visible*, p. 11.

Doane associates this type of white presumption with an overdetermined sense of individuality present in the thinking of white peoples.[14] He suggests that white people do not attribute any part of their accomplishments, situations or achievements to the fact of their whiteness; they instead think of such accomplishments as having been individually earned. Nancy Ditomaso furthers the argument by claiming that white people do not even attribute their accomplishments to the help of other white people: 'The focus on individual achievement rather than group relations has taken attention away from the power relations that exist between groups.'[15] In other words, because white people are convinced that their achievements result from their own individual meritoriousness, they overlook the degree to which their parents', neighbours' and teachers' income, influence and connections made achievements possible for them. As well, it can be argued that white people tend to overlook the degree to which the neighbourhoods in which they lived created opportunities for them via the schools they attended, the recommendations they received from white peoples who had also had numerous opportunities, and more. Thus, scholars find that because collective white assistance is so thoroughly embedded and unnamed in society, 'whites can easily point to the things they had to do to get to their current places in life, but they do not at the same time as easily recall the group basis of their life outcomes'.[16] Holden Caulfield claims in the long opening paragraph of the novel that he is bored by storytelling that includes information about one's childhood, one's parents and their occupations: 'That stuff bores me [. . .] Besides, I'm not going to tell you my whole goddam autobiography or anything' (Ch. 1, p. 1). Reading Holden's boredom and protectiveness with an eye to understanding his particular whiteness, we can begin to read even his own fatigue as representative of a type of privilege: the privilege to 'not tell' and to 'withhold'. He refuses to talk about his parents and the life they have provided for him. As a white man in American society, Holden presumes he has a right to privacy to be completely determined by him. He thus makes it clear to us that he will tell us only what he wants to tell us.

Along with the right to privacy as expressed by the choice to 'not tell', Holden also supports the choice to 'not think too much'. At the beginning of Chapter 2, Holden asks us to witness a Saturday visit to his teacher's house for hot chocolate, but he suggests that we not think about Mr Spencer and his ageing process too much. Besides the teacher's bad posture and his age, one of the characterising details that Holden shares about Mr Spencer is the man's 'old beat-up Navajo blanket that he and Mrs. Spencer'd bought off some Indian in Yellowstone Park' (Ch. 2, p. 6). If we don't think about it too much, as Holden suggests, we don't think about or discuss the socio-cultural aspects of the Navajo rug purchase. We don't think about the fact that Yellowstone Park was the USA's first national park, established in 1872, and that the National Park Service throughout the USA was dealing with great resistance from American Indians whose lands were

---

14 Doane, in Doane and Eduardo Bonilla-Silva, *White Out*, p. 14.
15 Nancy Ditomaso, Rochelle Parks-Yancy and Corinne Post, 'White Views of Civil Rights: Color Blindness and Equal Opportunity', in Doane and Bonilla-Silva, *White Out*, p. 190.
16 Doane, in Doane and Eduardo Bonilla-Silva, *White Out*, p. 191.

sometimes included proprietarily in the broad plans for the national parks.[17] Babb claims that white people often conflate the idea of Americanness with their own whiteness, thus implying that:

> whites have a proprietary right to national resources and the allocation of these resources. While the legal privileging of whiteness has been overturned through statutes banning segregation, advocating fair housing practices, and urging equal employment, more difficult to overturn are the values and attitudes that accomplish in principle what the law disallows, values and attitudes that persist as legacies of a constructed whiteness.[18]

The reader is not encouraged to think about the role of the white man in the confinement of Indian tribes on reservations, or the commodification of Indian material goods such as blankets. The 'beat-up blanket' that warms Mr Spencer is not presented as a desirable commodity of Indian culture. The Indian who made the blanket is not named in the manner typical for artists and artisans who have handcrafted pieces of work: he/she is simply referred to generically as 'some Indian'. The person's only identifiable marker is tribal. The Navajo has become aligned in the story only with his/her material product. Mr Spencer has literally surrounded himself with a cultural byproduct of the ongoing reality of American Indians, and yet no such reality is apparent to any of the white people visiting Mr Spencer, including Holden Caulfield. Once again, we must note that the cultural perceptions of Holden Caulfield are extremely narrow and particular: they are not universal in their wisdom, nor are they critical perceptions of the immediate world that surrounds him. Salinger provides Holden's tale with an Indian commodity to adorn a white story. The Indian blanket is not a semiotic sign that initiates a critique from Holden; rather, it is a multicultural prop designed as backdrop to the story of white Mr Spencer's travels.

Similar examples of aligning Indians with their commodities or their stereotyped behaviours exist throughout the novel: in Chapter 16, as Holden walks toward the Museum of Natural History, he remembers his school field trips to the museum. His memories are fraught with the 'stuff' that Indians made. He remembers a long war canoe and 'about twenty Indians' paddling the canoe and 'standing around looking tough' (Ch. 16, p. 109). Specifically he recounts the mask of a witch doctor, Indians 'rubbing sticks together', and a 'squaw weaving a blanket' (Ch. 16, p. 109). Salinger writes the 'squaw' as an exotic Other when he has Holden remember the erotic qualities of her breasts. Holden offers only the following analysis of these artifact memories: 'Certain things they should stay the way they are. You ought to be able to stick them in one of these big glass cases and just leave them alone' (Ch. 16, p. 110). Holden clearly assumes that what can be valued about 'certain things' such as Indian life is containable. And even though the museum did show a movie of Columbus discovering America, Holden

---

17   National Park Service, 'Making It Work: Monument Development 1910–1955' in US Department of the Interior, *An Administrative History of Rainbow Bridge*, 2003, <http://www.nps.gov/rabr/adhi/adhi4.htm>.
18   Babb, *Whiteness Visible*, p. 5.

claims that 'nobody gave too much of a damn about old Columbus' (Ch. 16, p. 108). Michael Cowan argues that Holden's narrative in this chapter is locked into 'museum discourse'.[19] He claims that when Holden is discussing the Indians and the Inuit of Chapter 16, his discourse reveals 'the role of modern ethno-graphic museums in turning cultural processes and products into aesthetic objects and in creating cultural narratives that privilege and rationalize the power of the collectors'.[20] I would add to Cowan's argument that Holden also espouses a white discourse prevalent among people wanting to privilege the role of 'whites' in all aspects of the world's cultural undertakings. Similar generalisations regarding Others and Otherness that clearly distinguish Holden's perceptions as 'white' abound in *Catcher*.

In Chapter 13, Holden meets a drunk Cuban man coming out of a 'dumpy looking bar' who has 'stinking breath' (p. 82); in Chapter 16, he wants to buy a record sung by 'this colored girl singer, Estelle Fletcher' (p. 104) who sings the song in a 'very Dixieland and whorehouse' style (p. 104); in Chapter 19, he is stunned by an acquaintance's interest in a Chinese girl, and his mind focuses on the stereotypical sexual renown of Chinese girls (pp. 132–3); and, in Chapter 25, he notices a 'colored' kid at Phoebe's school (p. 180). Holden's use of stereotypes to 'other' the racially diverse characters of the novel serves to define his whiteness without ever naming himself as white in these particular instances. We know that he is not-Cuban because the Cuban man is identified in opposition to himself. We know that Holden is not coloured because he clearly associates the 'colored' singer's voice with the south and with stereotyped eroticism and because he feels compelled to name the skin of the boy at Phoebe's school as 'colored'. Readers are expected to assume that a white boy in the hallway of Phoebe's school would not be labelled as a white boy, but would instead, because he is the same 'normative' race as Holden, be described simply as a boy. We know that Holden is not-Chinese because he has to name and clarify the race of the girl that his friend describes, thus expecting the readers to understand that his own whiteness does not need such explanation. Lipsitz claims that 'the recurrence of racial stereotypes in art and in life [. . .] and the white fascination with certain notions of primitive authenticity among communities of color, all testify to the white investment in images that whites themselves have created about people of color'.[21]

Another form of Othering that occurs in *Catcher* is that within the institutions described by Holden. Holden tells us that when he was in school, he studied only literature and history that promoted a European understanding of history and culture. In Chapter 15, Holden claims: 'Most of the time we were on the Anglo-Saxons, Beowulf, and old Grendel, and Lord Randal My Son and all those things. But we had to read outside books for extra credit once in a while' (Ch. 15, p. 100). In relaying his curriculum, Holden reveals that most educational time was spent in studying European literature and that anything other than that had

19 Michael Cowan, 'Holden's Museum Pieces: Narrator and Nominal Audience in *The Catcher in the Rye*', in Jack Salzman (ed.), *New Essays on The Catcher in the Rye*, Cambridge: Cambridge University Press, 1991, p. 36.
20 Cowan, in Salzman, *New Essays*, p. 54n.
21 George Lipsitz, *The Possessive Investment in Whiteness: How White People Profit from Identity Politics*, Philadelphia, Pa.: Temple University Press, 1998, p. 118.

to be studied on one's own time. Thus, the standard curriculum supported the white assumptions of white Americans, while people were free to read other literatures only when they remained external to the established curriculum. Babb describes such curricula as programming designed to assure white people that they are the authentic peoples.[22] She writes that 'the academic missions of most schools [. . .] employed a variety of subject matters to inculcate the history, values, visions, and consequences of only one segment of American society'.[23] The curricula in the schools that Holden attended promoted material that grounded its white readers as active participants in all aspects of culture and civilisation. The same curricula marginalised or labelled as 'extra' all educational subject matter and texts not relevant to the white experience.

In Chapter 7, Holden Caulfield becomes determined to leave Pencey in the middle of the night. He decides to 'take a room in a hotel in New York – some very inexpensive hotel and all – and just take it easy till Wednesday' (Ch. 7, p. 45). In 1951, the average hotel rate across the country was five dollars and ninety-one cents.[24] Assuming that Holden could attain an 'inexpensive' hotel room in New York, even on the West Side, he would still have more money than most sixteen-year-old people of colour in New York: 'By the 1950s, black workers aged twenty-four to forty-four faced unemployment levels three times those confronting their white counterparts.'[25] Holden is only sixteen; he has money, and he does not have to work for it: 'Holden seems to exist in a world almost entirely composed of leisure pursuits. We hardly ever see him in a context of anything that might be called work, which in his case would be academic study.'[26] Holden's leisure time is supported by the financial flow that comes from his heritage as a white man; he receives his money from his grandmother in 'wads' (Ch. 7, p. 46) that he doesn't even count, and yet he does not articulate the connection between his white racial heritage, his leisure time and the material goods of his life.

In addition to the hotel room, he has enough money to buy a train ticket, ham and Swiss-cheese sandwiches, four magazines, a five-dollar record for his sister, a malted; enough to make phone calls from phone booths, to see a matinee, to go to Radio City Music Hall and to give ten dollars to the nuns at the end of Chapter 15. Doane reminds us that: 'Because whites tend not to see themselves in racial terms and not to recognize the advantages that whites enjoy in American society, this promotes a worldview that emphasized *individualistic* explanations for social and economic achievement, as if the individualism of white privilege was a universal attribute.'[27] Holden thinks that people are individualistically expressed through the material items they are able to display. In Chapter 15, he relays to the reader his thoughts and feelings about cheap suitcases. He says: 'It isn't important, I know, but I hate it when somebody has cheap suitcases. It sounds terrible to say

22 Babb, *Whiteness Visible*, p. 156.
23 Babb, *Whiteness Visible*, pp. 157–8.
24 American Hotel and Lodging Association, *History of Lodging*, 2005, <http://www.ahma.com/products_lodging_history.asp>.
25 Lipsitz, *The Possessive Investment in Whiteness*, p. 30.
26 Christopher Brookeman, 'Pencey Preppy: Cultural Codes in *The Catcher in the Rye*', in Salzman, *New Essays*, p. 63.
27 Doane, in Doane and Eduardo Bonilla-Silva, *White Out*, p. 14.

it, but I even get to hate somebody, just *looking at them*, if they have cheap suitcases with them' (Ch. 15, p. 97). Holden knows it's a deplorable thing to value people according to their acquisitions, but at the same time, his sense that an individual is represented by such items as a suitcase is deeply embedded in his socio-racial sense of how the world works. Babb suggests that we can better understand the way whiteness exhibits its power in American society when we think of it 'not solely as a biological category of pigmentation or hair texture, but rather as a means through which certain individuals are granted greater degrees of social acceptance and access than are other individuals'.[28] Thinking in the way that Babb encourages enables us to see that it does not occur to Holden that many individuals do not have the same choices as he has because they do not have the same socio-economic or skin privileges, nor do they have access to the social knowledge and acceptance that he takes for granted.

To Holden, all choices are ones made individually. When he walks forty-one blocks to his hotel through the night streets of New York, it is not because he has run out of money, nor because a cab refused to stop for him due to his race. He simply chooses to walk. At the beginning of Chapter 13, he tells us that he walks because 'sometimes you get tired of riding in taxicabs the same way you get tired riding in elevators' (Ch. 13, p. 80). The 'you' in this sentence presumes that Holden's readers are like him: perfectly capable of paying for numerous taxi rides across town and of having a cab stop for 'us' because of our non-threatening skin colour.

He does not know it fully, but Holden is part of the elite white hegemony that maintains the racialised social system in the USA. J. D. Salinger 'was interested in the hypocrisy of human nature, yet he was also drawn to the urbane, affluent lifestyle of the WASP'.[29] Thus, he creates a Holden as a young man who wants to separate from the social elitism of Pencey Prep, but he also writes a Holden who is unaware of the role that his whiteness plays in his own hypocrisy. Salinger may have thought that the hypocrisy might account for the emptiness he perceived at the centre of many affluent lives, and he was probably correct. However, I would also add that the nervous sensations that accompany Holden throughout the novel also resonate with the racialised social change evident throughout New York and the USA at the time.

One way to understand Holden's ultimate nervous breakdown is as a reaction to his awareness that in the new racialised world system, the white man will experience a great deal of instability. Babb theorises that:

> While the ideology that privileges white skin served many in the past, today it is problematic, for it limits its beneficiaries to an increasingly nescient and narrow sphere. Sequestered in a cloistered space that by degrees grows increasingly stifling, many are often unaware of its constraining nature. This ideology encourages them to live in their diverse world handicapped by an ignorance of the other cultures, traditions, and perspectives that constitute the majority of their world.[30]

28 Babb, *Whiteness Visible*, p. 3.
29 Alexander, *Salinger*, p. 29.
30 Babb, *Whiteness Visible*, p. 171.

At the end of *Catcher*, Holden is indeed sequestered, but he is not yet thinking too much about his 'sickness'. He misses his white buddies at the school, and he wishes he had maintained more of his privacy throughout the telling of his story. Thus, he faces his nascent experiences of the world with a rekindling of individualism. He recommits to his right to privacy, and in the very last paragraph of the novel, he insists on his inability to think: 'If you want to know the truth, I don't *know* what I think about it (Ch. 26, p. 192). In the world of this mid-century young, white, elite male, it is wholly better to not think and not tell, than it is to participate knowingly and actively in a complex racialised social system.

Pia Livia Hekanaho, '"Queering *Catcher*": flits, straights, and other morons'

Pia Livia Hekanaho lectures at the Institute of Art Research at the University of Helsinki and is a research fellow for the project 'Porn Academy' funded by the Academy of Finland. She has published articles in Finnish and English on queer theory and representations of masculinity in the works of Marguerite Yourcenar and Evelyn Waugh. She is currently writing a book on queer readings of Yourcenar. Like Duane Edwards (see Critical history, **pp. 57–8**), Livia Hekanaho offers a reading of *Catcher* that suggests that some of Holden's confusion about sexuality could stem from his complex desires for the same sex. Hekanaho develops Edwards' reading by employing queer theory to consider the ways in which Holden could be understood as a repressed gay adolescent who realises that he lives in a time and place in which same-sex desire is taboo. Queer theory, which is especially concerned with identity in relation to sex and gender, has been developing since the early 1990s and is particularly associated with the work of theorists Michel Foucault and Judith Butler. It takes issue with the conventional perceptions that sex (male/female) is biologically determined, that gender (masculine/feminine) is in turn determined by sex and that sexuality (hetero-homosexual) is similarly a fixed 'binary' (opposed pair) with predetermined links to sex and gender. Queer theory seeks to break or destabilise the assumed connections between gender, sex and desire by suggesting that all of these are characterised by fluidity rather than fixity. Queer theory also recognises that perceptions of sexual identity are socially constructed and differ across time and place. In post-war America, homosexuality was considered deviant and unspeakable: gay men and lesbians could not be open about their sexuality for fear of social condemnation. Homosexuality threatened to undermine traditional gender roles (because, for example, masculinity was equated with heterosexuality) and, as noted in Texts and contexts (**pp. 73–5**), rigid gender stereotypes were strongly approved in post-war America. Recognising this, Hekanaho's essay shows how Holden, as an adolescent in the 1950s, would have great difficulty coming to terms with his sexual identity: if the rituals of heterosexuality were difficult to understand, perceptions of same-sex desire were even more confused by prejudice and ignorance. Using queer theory to interpret Holden's narrative, Hekanaho offers in this essay a new understanding of Holden's sexuality. That Holden himself is apparently unaware of his potential for homosexual orientation affirms the unspeakable and unrecognised aspects of homosexual identity in his place and time.

Pia Livia Hekanaho, 'Queering *Catcher*: flits, straights, and other morons'

While previous readings of *The Catcher in the Rye* have often approached it as a *Bildungsroman* (a coming-of-age novel), and stressed themes like white male anger or post-war anti-bourgeois rebellion, my reading of the novel focuses on the depiction of non-hegemonic masculinity and sexualities. Making a queer reading of a novel or, indeed, the whole idea of 'queering' anything gives rise to various expectations. In my queering act, I am concerned with the leaking boundaries of 'straight' (heterosexual) masculinity and the queer identities that may lie beyond those boundaries. Instead of focusing on ways in which the novel represents deviations from straight male sexuality, I will address the queer topic of straightness, and the closely knit bond between straightness and the 'deviant' margins. Indeed, marginal and queer identities and positions are necessary for defining categories such as straightness, 'normality' or heteronormativity (the social rules that establish that heterosexuality is both natural and ideal). As a process, queering destabilises sexual identity categories and finds 'queer spaces', points of ambiguity and alternative perspectives, in language and culture.

The word 'queer' has historically signified something strange and, more specifically, queer has been used to refer to an odd or weird person or thing. For queer theory, though, the most *fruit*ful part of the *freak*ish history of *queer* has been its long life as a derogatory word for a homosexual person. Queer is an old slang word which, like 'fruit', 'fag(got)', and 'fairy', is one of the various derogatory names applied to male homosexuals. 'Flit', the slang word for an effeminate gay man that *Catcher*'s protagonist Holden Caulfield uses, is a member of the same family. The adjective 'flitty' that frequents Holden's monologue originated in the 1950s. 'Gay', denoting a person with same-sex desire, emerged around 1930. According to Peter Nardi, 'flit' specifically indicated effeminacy, as did 'queen' and 'fairy', whereas 'a queer' was simply a person with an interest in same-sex relationships.[1]

As an academic discourse, queer theory emerged in the early 1990s; the term 'queer theory' was coined by Teresa de Lauretis in her introductory article in *differences* in 1991. Theorists borrowed the term from radical gender and sexual activism: in the discourse of political movements like ACT UP (an AIDS activist group) and Queer Nation, the old negative slang word 'queer' became a positive and empowering one. Queer came to signify 'positively and radically different',

---

1   Peter Nardi (ed.), *Gay Masculinities*, London: Sage, 2000, pp. 2–5.

not just 'gay or lesbian', which became less radical terms in the discourse of sexual politics. Queer is often understood to transgress the politics of assimilation that characterises the gay and lesbian movement. Tamsin Spargo notes that 'queer' can function as a noun, an adjective or a verb, but in each case it is defined against the 'normal' or normalising. Queer theory is a collection of intellectual engagements with the relations between sex, gender and sexual desire, as she succinctly puts it.[2]

The first volume of Michel Foucault's *The History of Sexuality* (1976) and its understanding of the role that social construction plays in the formation of sexualities had a strong influence on the emergent queer theory. Queer theorists understand the intertwined systems of sexuality and gender as historically constructed networks of knowledge and power. Two important works of queer theory appeared in 1990. One was *Gender Trouble*, in which Judith Butler gave a central position to lesbian subcultures when exploring the 'performativity' of gender, suggesting that gender roles are not given or natural, but are learned and performed by constant reiteration. The other key text was Eve Kosofsky Sedgwick's ground-breaking *Epistemology of the Closet*, which focused on the cultural centrality of the demarcation line between male homosexuality and heterosexuality and the huge cultural investment in sexual knowledge and secrecy that characterises modernity in certain societies, including the USA. Sexual subcultures, subversive identities and non-normative genders have been prominent areas of queer studies, as have questions about the history of homosexuality or the historical construction of different sexualities, and the issue of heteronormativity.

Scrutinising anti-hegemonic genders and sexualities has inspired queer scholars to question normative, hegemonic and largely naturalised identities. Masculinity studies emerged from feminist studies and, since the queer turn in gender theory, masculinity has been explored in both men and women, as shown in the concept of *female masculinity*, coined by Judith Halberstam in her 1998 book of the same name. Critical and queer race theory has understood whiteness, too, as a constructed identity formation and one of the latest interests among queer scholars has been the study of heterosexuality, or straightness, as a cultural construction much like all other sexualities which, until now, have largely been seen as deviations from heterosexuality. Consequently, white straight male masculinity is an emerging issue in queer studies, and *The Catcher in the Rye*, perhaps surprisingly, turns out to be quite a catch for a reader willing to queer this classic and controversial novel.

Holden Caulfield, the narrator, is a sixteen- or seventeen-year-old white male. We also know that he is the second oldest child of a wealthy Manhattan family and that he has attended – with deplorable lack of success – quite a few of the finest prep schools in the country, the latest of which is Pencey Prep. Holden's narration starts and ends with his thoughts on the homosocial (a term used to describe social bonds between persons of same sex) community of adolescent males at Pencey.[3] However, while we can be certain of his age, race, gender and

2   Tamsin Spargo, *Foucault and Queer Theory*, Cambridge: Icon Books, 2000, pp. 8–9.
3   Eve Kosofsky Sedgwick, *Between Men: English Literature and Male Homosocial Desire*, New York: Columbia University Press, 1985, pp. 1–2.

middle-class status, Holden's sexuality seems more ambiguous: is his odyssey the story of a young, white *straight* male?

In the novel, the recurrent motif of the ambiguity of sexual identity heightens the ambivalence of clear-cut identity categories. The blurred line between normative and non-normative male sexuality, or gay and straight desires and social roles, are a crucial part of Holden's story. In his narration, Holden constantly uses various images of difference or deviancy. He frequently mentions 'flits' and 'perverts', the names he chooses for the central counter-identities that inform his representation of manhood. After a nocturnal incident with Mr Antolini, his former English teacher, interpreted by Holden as a homosexual act, he states that something 'perverty like that' has happened to him 'about twenty times' since he was a kid; and he 'can't stand it' (Ch. 24, p. 174). According to Duane Edwards, Holden's reaction to Mr Antolini's gesture indicates that 'he is projecting his desire for homosexual expression onto Antolini'.[4] The same might be said about his interaction with Carl Luce, his former student adviser, whom he encounters in the Wicker Bar of the 'swanky' Seton Hotel (Ch. 19, pp. 128–34). A queer reading gives space to Holden's ambivalent sexuality, interpreting it as a constant oscillation between the cultural patterns of straightness, sexual difference and counter-cultural ways of life, instead of just naming him immature or unbalanced.

Holden finds normative masculinity repellent, but alternative ways of being a man in the post-war American social setting hold no attraction for him either. His constant movement between desire and repulsion in relation to masculinity and sexuality may be interpreted as a sign of queer diversity. Holden's vision of masculinity vacillates between images of safe but suffocating straight 'normality' and that of 'deviant' sexuality, which only seems another dead end. The central figures of his anxiety are closeted gay men. They might be anywhere, anyone might turn into one, and the threat of queerness is present everywhere in the form of a *passing* gay man (that is, a man who is understood to be heterosexual but is actually homosexual). Ultimately, as Holden fears, the closet only seems to offer another set of anxieties and restrictions, which are just different from the version offered by straight life. In the novel, the narrated ambivalence about sexuality and the relational character of 'normality' underline the constructedness of masculinity identified by various queer theorists. Queer theory has drawn heavily on psychoanalysis for its understanding of the formation of masculine identity. For example, as Butler argues, all identity formations, including masculinity and straightness, are shaped by repression. The boundaries which shape hegemonic masculinity are defined by culturally and socially enforced fears of 'castrated', unmanly gender identities, femininity, and 'abhorrent' images of sexual deviancy. The most frightening feature of a 'flit' is not, in the terms of this theory, his male–male desire, but his effeminacy.

Holden describes the seedy Edmont Hotel as being 'full of perverts and morons; screwballs all over the place' (Ch. 9, p. 54). He finds the sight of activities that represent a range of genders and sexualities both alluring and abhorrent at the same time. This is especially evident when Holden reports his voyeuristic interest in the solitary pleasures of a male transvestite whose dressing up he observes

---

4   Edwards, in Salzberg, *Critical Essays*, p. 154.

through a hotel window, and the kinky sexual games of a straight couple (Ch. 9, pp. 55–6). As much as the transvestite's solitary pleasure shocks Holden, his description nonetheless conveys a strong feeling of hidden but intense enjoyment. Non-hegemonic masculinity hovers in the background of the narrative in the shape of an 'Otherness' (a marked difference from the dominant norm) that simultaneously troubles and fascinates Holden. The transvestite is recognisably Other, but the threat of invisible, all-pervasive, closeted gayness is a different matter. In fact, the anti-normative sexual pleasure the guests display make Holden think of Stradlater, his room-mate at Pencey and the object of his ambivalent feelings.

Hints of male homosexuality recur in Holden's story as he frequents 'mixed' bars and nightclubs. He panics at the possibility of suddenly turning gay himself and the presence of 'flitty', deviant masculinity pervades his narrative. 'Flits' and 'perverts' form the boundary against which he defines the performance of masculinity that he feels is demanded of an adult male. In Chapter 19, he gives a great deal of thought to the topic of homosexuality, or 'flits and lesbians' (Ch. 19, p. 129). The abhorring frailty of straight masculinity becomes evident when Holden favourably remembers his former student adviser Carl Luce's exposures of the disquieting omnipresence of homosexuality:

> He said it didn't matter if a guy was married or not. He said half the married guys in the world were flits and didn't even know it. He said you could turn into one practically overnight, if you had all the traits and all. He used to scare the hell out of us. I kept waiting to turn into a flit or something. The funny thing about old Luce, I used to think he was sort of flitty himself, in a way.
>
> (Ch. 19, p. 129)

Holden has his doubts about Luce, whose tendency to find opportunities to 'goose the hell out of you' and encourage intimate chats in the bathroom, coupled with his vast interest and knowledge of 'perverts' and 'closet cases' make him a potential 'flit' (Ch. 19, p. 129). Yet Holden himself has a suggestive history, since he has some knowledge of 'real flits' (Ch. 19, p. 129) and, in his narrative, the question of knowing oneself and finding out the sexual secrets of others are related. Holden, indeed, is the one who seeks out the possibly gay characters in the story, namely Carl Luce and Mr Antolini; he (Holden) is the aggressor (the active one in seeking out company) if there is one, as Edwards puts it.[5] Holden is attracted to – and attracts – gay men.

In *Between Men* (1985), Sedgwick describes the term 'homosocial' as a neologism (a new word), formed by analogy with 'homosexual', but meant to be distinguished from that. Homosociality can be applied to such activities as 'male bonding', which may even be characterised by intense homophobia (fear and hatred of homosexuals). However, Sedgwick suggests that homosociality and homosexuality are actually parts of the same continuum, since the area of homosociality belongs to the orbit of desire, the potentially erotic. According to

---

5 Edwards, in Salzberg, *Critical Essays*, pp. 153–4.

Sedgwick: 'In any male-dominated society, there is a special relationship between male homosocial (*including* homosexual) desire and the structures for maintaining and transmitting patriarchal power.'[6] Social and educational institutions that pass on traditions, culture and class-based attitudes indoctrinate young males with forms of hegemonic masculinity by maintaining the primary status of homosocial relationships. The inner and social worlds depicted in the novel are strongly homosocial. Holden's narration is dominated by his social and emotional relations to boys, men, masculine ideals and abject figures such as 'flits' and 'perverts'.

Boys' schools are an archetypal example of a male homosocial environment and form a significant milieu in Holden's narrative. His narrative starts and ends with memories of two jocks from Pencey Prep, Stradlater and Ackley, whom he acknowledges missing. Indeed, Chapter 4 of the novel features a long description of Holden's interaction with Stradlater, his overtly (and stereotypically) masculine roommate. The scene in the bathroom in which Holden keeps the shaving Stradlater company indicates male–male intimacy filled with jealous tension. Their wrestling match is loaded with Holden's simultaneous identification with and desire for Stradlater, who is going on a date with Jane Gallagher, a girl Holden knows and likes. Sedgwick suggests that a triangular model of 'rivalry' of two men over a woman is a recurrent feature of the Western intellectual tradition. In any erotic contest, the bonds of 'rivalry' and 'love' are equally powerful and in many senses equivalent. In *Catcher*, we may discern echoes of this triangle in Holden's jealousy towards Stradlater and Jane. The idea of Stradlater being sexually intimate with Jane makes Holden anxious: the reader might speculate as to whether the cause of his nauseating anxiety is his jealousy of Jane or of Stradlater. Or, indeed, does Holden in fact identify with Jane Gallagher? Instead of identifying with the standard role of masculine predator, he may see himself in the feminine role of the prey.

Holden shows more sibling-like camaraderie than desire towards his girlfriends. Significantly, he shuns the idea of sexual activity with girls, and the idea of having sex with Sunny, the young prostitute at the hotel, is quite paralysing to him. Partly, the explanation may be the repulsiveness of the whole setting, but it might also be that he experiences some kind of identification with the girl. Holden understands that the feminine role in the mating game of the 1950s is a victimised position, and the novel makes clear that he empathises with the vulnerable and feels more comfortable with the role of protector than with that of sexual predator. To Holden, straight masculinity seems to signify a domineering position in a biased game, and he is neither willing nor able to play that part.

Maurice, the bellboy, punches Holden when he refuses to give him more money. Significantly, this happens right after Holden has talked himself out of having sex with Sunny who Maurice is pimping. As in the bathroom scene at Pencey, a scene of physical intimacy and sexual tension leads to a fight, and Maurice may be read as a kind of surrogate version of Stradlater. Maurice and Stradlater are older and more aggressive than Holden and they are both figured as sexually experienced – and exploitative – in a way that Holden refuses to emulate. It is remarkable that, apart from Jane, the female characters most meaningful to Holden are his

6   Sedgwick, *Between Men*, p. 25.

pre-pubescent sister Phoebe and two Catholic nuns who he happens to run into; he has no sexual intimacy with any of these female figures. Except for Phoebe, the characters that move or trouble Holden emotionally or with whom he experiences physical and emotional intimacy are male.

Holden's distaste for hegemonic masculinity is apparent when he analyses the conventional role of a lawyer which, in fact, his father happens to inhabit: 'All you do is make a lot of dough and play golf and play bridge and buy cars and drink Martinis and look like a hot-shot' (Ch. 22, p. 155). By contrast, the recurrent figure of the homosexual and Holden's doomed efforts at remaining an adolescent indefinitely, represent ambiguous chances to evade the restrictions of a normative masculine role. Young James Castle and Mr Antolini, Holden's former English teacher, are central figures of non-hegemonic masculinity. In his narrative, Holden associates James Castle with Mr Antolini. James was a quiet boy at Elkton Hills, killed by bullies: a 'skinny little weak-looking guy, with wrists about as big as pencils' (Ch. 22, p. 153). When James jumped out of the window, it was Mr Antolini who picked up his body and carried him to the infirmary. In Holden's narrative, James is a frightening example of failed, non-hegemonic masculinity: a shy and fragile boy who dies when abused by 'dirty bastards' (Ch. 22, p. 153). His uprising ends in defeat and, to Holden, the whole scenario suggests that failing the test of hegemonic masculinity leads to peril, even death. Holden detests the idea of hegemonic masculinity, but it also proves to be difficult to find any successful role models for non-hegemonic masculinity.

Mr Antolini has quit Elkton Hills and moved on to teaching English at New York University. He has married a wealthy older woman, and they lead a life rich with artistic friends and strong drinks. Mr Antolini's ambivalent character epitomises Holden's anxieties about masculinity and sexuality. The former teacher is his hero in that he has not sold out to bourgeois conformity, but he shocks Holden with his gesture of intimacy the night Holden sleeps at his apartment. Holden awakens suddenly to find the drunken Mr Antolini sitting on the floor and petting his head. Disillusioned, Holden is seized by homophobic panic, though the ultimate motivation behind Mr Antolini's gesture remains ambivalent. Afterwards, Holden has doubts as to whether he interpreted the situation correctly, but Mr Antolini's uneasiness and strained casualness reveal that he is as frightened as Holden:

> 'What the hellya *doing*?' I said.
> 'Nothing! I'm simply sitting here, admiring–'
> 'What're ya *doing*, anyway?' I said over again. I didn't know *what* the hell to say – I mean I was embarrassed as hell.
> 'How 'bout keeping your voice down? I'm simply sitting here–'
> (Ch. 24, pp. 172–3)

Ambiguity in the area of sexual identity is, in fact, a feature that Holden shares with the supposedly gay characters in the novel, and the dubious episode with Mr Antolini underlines the crucial theme of ambivalence. As with Carl Luce, Holden's former student adviser, the implication of closeted gayness is strong around Mr Antolini. Their socially and economically beneficial relationships with older women suggest their closeted homosexuality, as does Luce's omniscience about visible and invisible flits. Duane Edwards, too, notes how 'Carl Luce, Mr Antolini and Holden are linked by their sexual interest in older women'.[7] While on the train to New York, Holden encounters Mrs Morrow, forty-five-year-old mother of his schoolmate, and tries clumsily to flirt with her (Ch. 8, pp. 47–52).

A network of suggestions link Holden to the gay characters in the story. Holden's interest in all aspects of anti-normative sexuality is always present in his narration, and he seems to find pleasure in his voyeuristic tendencies, too, enjoying the role of onlooker. The crucial act of recognition – or misrecognition – occurs when Mr Antolini, addressing Holden as a 'handsome' and 'a very, very strange boy', *recognises* him, correctly or not, as a fellow queer (Ch. 24, pp. 172–3). The most crucial questions may not be whether Mr Antolini is really a closeted gay man or not, or the accuracy of his recognition of a queer kid in the making. Even a possible misperception (Mr Antolini's or a reader's) may have value: Mr Antolini addressing Holden as a queer peer makes it inevitable that Holden sees himself as one, at least temporarily. In spite of the ambivalence of these recognitions, they may well open new interpretative horizons for Holden: new possibilities and modes of being and becoming. Mr Antolini's advice to Holden is rather ambiguous in tone, and to a queer eye it could be read as survival kit designed to help a queer kid:

> Many, many men have been just as troubled morally and spiritually as you are right now. Happily, some of them kept record of their troubles. You'll learn from them – if you want to. Just as someday, if you have something to offer, someone will learn from you. It's a beautiful reciprocal arrangement. And it isn't education. It's history. It's poetry.
>
> (Ch. 24, p. 170)

Mr Antolini's speech about scholarly fellowship that transcends history seems to be open to a queer reading. It is reminiscent of the concept of a gay community that ensures that novices learn the coded language and behaviour of the closeted era. In part, becoming gay in a repressive era like the 1950s in America meant learning to feel and desire differently without conventional role models or social affirmation. While Holden leaves his mentor's home in a state of homosexual panic, later on, he wonders whether he overreacted. He realises that Mr Antolini might indeed be gay and yet still be a caring person with integrity and understanding.

Holden's first reaction to Mr Antolini's mentoring was repudiation, but by the end of the novel it is apparent that he has complied, in a sense, with his mentor's advice: he is working on his psyche while staying in an institution after a nervous breakdown. He is also reconciled to the necessity of gaining a solid education to back up his critical and creative potential. Holden's narrative starts in a homosocial milieu, an all-boys' school, and ends with him reporting that he misses male camaraderie: 'About all I know is, I sort of *miss* everybody I told about. Even old Stradlater and Ackley, for instance. I think I even miss that goddam Maurice. It's funny. Don't ever tell anybody anything. If you do, you start missing everybody' (Ch. 26, p. 192).

---

7   Edwards, in Salzberg, *Critical Essays*, pp. 153, 157, n. 19.

What connects Stradlater, Ackley and Maurice is the awkward intimacy that Holden has felt with them. In the case of Stradlater and his surrogate, the bell-boy Maurice, the physical intimacy is achieved through fighting, a violent act which nonetheless demands closeness and engagement. At the end of his story, Holden reveals something about his feelings of emotional intimacy and the names he mentions in addition to his brother, D. B., are three archetypes of straight masculinity, who have stirred his affections.

The Catcher in the Rye oscillates between straightness and queerness, set in the closeted gay space of the American 1950s. What might be read as a *Bildungsroman* about a white, middle-class heterosexual male can just as well be read as the subtle coming-out story of a queer youngster. The movement between these alternate frames of reference mirrors the evasiveness and ambiguity that mark the closeted discourses of non-normative desires. Bernard S. Oldsey was certainly not making a queer reading in 1961 while commenting on the ambiguous nature of Holden's encounter with Mr Antolini, but he perceptively identifies the ambiguity that is characteristic of all Holden's sexual feelings and experiences.[8] The blurred boundaries between the homosocial and the homosexual, between gay and straight versions of masculinity, allow us to read Holden Caulfield as an adolescent coming to terms with his sexuality as a significant aspect of the man he will become. As Holden says, with sex 'you never know *where* the hell you are' (Ch. 9, p. 56). Perhaps that is why it is not too difficult to 'queer' *The Catcher in the Rye*.

8   Bernard S. Oldsey, 'The Movies in the Rye', in Salzberg, *Critical Essays*, p. 97.

Denis Jonnes, 'Trauma, mourning and self-(re)fashioning in
The Catcher in the Rye'

Denis Jonnes is Professor of English and Cultural Studies at Kitakyushu University, Japan. His publications include a book, *The Matrix of Narrative: Family Systems and the Semiotics of Story* (1990) and articles on Arthur Miller, Tennessee Williams, Jack Kerouac, Sylvia Plath and Flannery O'Connor. He is currently working on a book on 'generational difference' in post-war American fiction and drama. Jonnes's essay on *The Catcher in the Rye* makes use of trauma theory, which developed from Sigmund Freud's late-nineteenth-century formulation of the impact on a person of repressed or unspeakable experience. Such experience is so painful that it is 'buried' in the unconscious, shaping the individual's responses to subsequent experience without being recognised or healed. This psychoanalytical understanding has been developed in recent years by other theorists and has been applied to the experiences of Holocaust survivors; it is now used increasingly to interpret a wide range of texts. Traumatic experience is subjective, which is to say that although a traumatised subject will have lived through an event that has shaped her/him in profound ways, it is not possible to measure or anticipate the impact of an event on an individual. The complexity of human responses means that one person can cope with what another may find unbearable and damaging. Trauma may be experienced in many different circumstances – in childhood, for example, or war, or in an unexpected event that is unique to an individual. However it happens, the shock of trauma can cause a range of psychological problems including gaps in memory, uncontrollable reactions, anxiety and depression. Unlike a period of stress, trauma permanently damages an individual's capacity to cope with living, often causing fragmentation in her/his psychic well-being. As a result, aspects of a person's experience are 'missing' because they are too painful for the individual to acknowledge and have been blocked out; this blocked or repressed trauma cannot be escaped and tends to express itself in unmanageable reactions. The potential to heal trauma is offered by the creation of a personal narrative which retrieves the unspeakable experiences and restores them to their place in the individual's own life story. Interpreting a work of literature in light of trauma theory might mean reading the text for signs that a character or even the author is repressing trauma which is leaking into the narrative. This might be evidenced by what a character cannot say or do as much as by what he does, by a fragmented or unreliable narrative, or by a repetitive concern with an object, place, person or moment that is closely associated with the traumatic experience. Although reading a novel solely in relation to the biography of its author is often discouraged by literary critics, Jonnes here offers an illuminating reading of *Catcher* that links Salinger's experiences in the Second World War (see Texts and contexts, **pp. 4–5**) to Holden's inexpressible grief at the loss of Allie. In this case, reading the novel as 'trauma fiction' offers an insight into Holden's crisis: interpreting what he cannot say about his loss provides Jonnes with a way of understanding Holden's experiences. Thus, Holden can be seen both as a strategy for Salinger to work through his own war trauma and as a character in his own right, an adolescent struggling with a deep sense of loss that shapes the ways in which he responds to his situation.

Denis Jonnes, 'Trauma, mourning and self-(re)fashioning in *The Catcher in the Rye*: reinventing youth in Cold War America'

'The thing to listen for, every time, with a public confessor, is what he's *not* confessing to.'[1]

While any judgement about J. D. Salinger's achievement must rest on the merits of his published work, his place within American culture is inextricably intertwined with the act of self-silencing with which in the mid-1960s he terminated his career as a publishing author. Like a handful of his contemporaries – Kerouac, Ginsberg, Burroughs – Salinger has become an iconic figure, his fiction one element in the larger myth of a 'life' identified, in this instance, with invisibility and silence. But if Salinger has gone to extraordinary lengths to ensure his privacy, his silence has also come to be read, paradoxically, as a 'text' in its own right. Ian Hamilton has used the term 'sequel' to suggest that Salinger's silence can itself be viewed as an expressive act which, for all it does not say, has lent a stamp of authenticity to the published work.[2] Louis Menand notes that 'Holden's unhappiness [. . .] helped to encourage the sense, encouraged by Salinger's own later manner, that there was no distinction between Salinger and his characters'.[3] Given Salinger's own early claims about the sources of his fiction – notably, that Holden Caulfield was modelled on his own youth – and the extent to which *Catcher* has been read as prefiguring the subsequent life, the biography (or what we know of it) has perhaps more than incidental bearing for any critical account of the work. In 1954, in the

---

1   J. D. Salinger, *Seymour: An Introduction*, London: Heinemann, 1963, p. 195.
2   Hamilton, *In Search of J. D. Salinger*, p. 137.
3   Louis Menand, 'Holden at Fifty: *The Catcher in the Rye* and What it Spawned', *The New Yorker*, 1 October 2001, p. 86.

only interview he ever granted, Salinger told the editor of the Windsor (Vermont) High School newspaper, that 'My boyhood was very much the same as that of the boy in the book [*Catcher*]'.[4] But for all the speculation that has surrounded Salinger's silence, none of the explanations put forward have been particularly convincing, and what his silence signifies remains as much of an enigma today as it was forty years ago when Salinger disappeared from public view.

In contrast to the life, the impact of his novel has posed considerably less of a problem. For many years, critical opinion held the book to be one of the first shots fired across the bows of the 1950s Cold War consensus, Holden the prototype of the disaffected post-war teenager 'terrified of regimentation'.[5] But in relocating the novel within the ideological cross-currents of the Cold War, recent assessments have regarded the work as both more and less radical than the reading of the novel as 'indispensable manual' for disaffected youth.[6] For example, Alan Nadel has contended that Holden's verbal behaviour – inquisitorial and self-indicting – is more of a piece with the Cold War attack on the legacies of the 1930s than a call to arms to newly dissident youth.[7]

There is no evidence, however, to suggest that Salinger as a young man had links with leftist groups, and the episodes of grief and anxiety, the bouts of despair and rage which punctuate Holden's narrative can be more productively viewed in relation to events directly connected to Salinger's own life. An enthusiastic supporter of American entry into the war, he sought to enlist in mid-1941 before the USA was formally at war, but his attitudes towards the war and his response in the wake of Pearl Harbor – 'outrage' and a powerful desire to 'make a contribution' – would have been typical of the time.[8] Inducted in April 1942, he was assigned to an infantry intelligence unit which participated in the D-Day landings and major campaigns in the European theatre. Salinger continued to write throughout the war, much of this work explicitly in support of the war effort. Of the twenty-two stories which he published from 1940 to the end of 1945, half address war-related themes, mostly celebrating wartime heroism, army comradeship and awareness that sacrifice, while tragic, was necessary. In 'The Last Day of the Last Furlough', (1944) the protagonist proclaims his eagerness to defend the country against aggressors: 'I believe in this war [. . .] I believe in killing Nazis and Fascists and Japs because there's no other way that I know of.'[9] For readers familiar with Salinger's post-war work, the attitudes expressed here – completely at odds with the material and tone of the later fiction – can prove somewhat disconcerting. Salinger's claim that he refuses republication simply because these stories represent the 'gaucheries of youth' (his phrase when bringing suit in 1974 to ban a pirate edition) loses something of its credibility.[10]

Equally clear, however, is the transformation that occurred once Salinger had

4 Alexander, *Salinger*, pp. 177–8.
5 John Seelye, 'Holden in the Museum', in Jack Salzman (ed.), *New Essays on The Catcher in the Rye*, Cambridge: Cambridge University Press, 1991, p. 30.
6 Hamilton, *In Search of J. D. Salinger*, p. 155.
7 Alan Nadel, *Containment Culture: American Narratives, Postmodernism and the Atomic Age*, Durham, NC: Duke University Press, 1997, pp. 71–89.
8 Hamilton, *In Search of J. D. Salinger*, p. 69.
9 J. D. Salinger, 'The Last Day of the Last Furlough', *The Saturday Evening Post*, 15 July 1944, p. 10.
10 Alexander, *Salinger*, p. 250.

been exposed to combat. Even for a combat unit, Salinger's division suffered 'an unusually high number of dead and wounded', and in certain campaigns 'sixty casualties a day' was not unusual'.[11] Salinger himself, though never wounded, was hospitalised for psychiatric reasons following VE day. As Alexander observes, the war was an experience which changed Salinger's 'patriotic, almost romantic view of war and the military forever'.[12] Salinger's daughter, Margaret, has stressed that:

> While the war was often in the foreground of our family life, it was *always* in the background. It was the point of reference that defined everything else in relation to it. [. . .] As long as I've known him, my father has never taken being warm and dry and *not being shot at* for granted. [. . .] The constant presence of the war, as something not really over, pervaded the years I lived at home.[13]

But at issue was something more than simply the loss of 'romantic' illusions. Given what happens to his combat veterans in stories published after the war – the unnamed narrator (who suffers a breakdown) in 'For Esmé – With Love and Squalor' (1950), Seymour (who commits suicide) in 'A Perfect Day for Bananafish' (1948) – it can be surmised that Salinger's battlefield experience was truly nightmarish, something which could render one terminally unfit for civilian life. Given the psychic disabilities suffered by Salinger's fictional combatants, I would identify the experience of trauma – resulting from what Robert Jay Lifton refers to as a 'death encounter' which has become 'central to [one's] psychological experience' – as key to any reading of Salinger's work.[14] Indeed, Salinger's career is marked by an epochal divide centered in a personal and collective experience of trauma, which opened up as Americans took stock of the costs of victory and grasped the new strategic realities of the Cold War. Felman and Laub have referred to the Second World War as the 'watershed trauma of our times – not an event encapsulated in the past, but as a history which is essentially not over, a history whose repercussions are omnipresent'.[15] In the wake of massive casualties, the Holocaust and the atomic bombings of Hiroshima and Nagasaki, trauma was to become, as Granofsky asserts, the defining experience of the second half of the twentieth century – 'the shock at the destructive potential in human depravity given free rein by technology inconceivable before 1945' giving rise to what he has called the 'trauma novel'.[16]

While theorists are in general agreement about the factors precipitating trauma and its immediate effects – 'a psychologically distressing event outside the range of usual human experience generating intense fear, terror, and helplessness' – they also stress the complex responses on the part of victims seeking to come to grips

11 Alexander, *Salinger*, pp. 101–2.
12 Alexander, *Salinger*, p. 100.
13 Margaret A. Salinger, *Dream Catcher*, p. 44.
14 Cathy Caruth (ed.), *Trauma: Explorations in Memory*, Baltimore, Md.: Johns Hopkins University Press, 1995, p. 128.
15 Shoshana Felman and Dori Laub, *Testimony: Crises of Witnessing in Literature, Psychoanalysis, and History*, New York and London: Routledge, 1992, p. xiv.
16 Ronald Granofsky, *The Trauma Novel*, New York: Peter Lang, 1995, p. 11.

with traumatic shock.[17] As Kali Tal notes, the subject is under a compulsion to 'tell and retell the story of the traumatic experience, to make it "real" both to the victim and to the community'.[18] However, theorists have also observed how, under the impact of trauma, perception and memory are suspended: 'No trace of a registration of any kind is left in the psyche, instead, a void, a hole is found.'[19] Whitehead has emphasised, in a comment of relevance to Salinger and his subsequent lapse into silence, how the traumatic event is 'not fully acknowledged at the time it occurs [. . .] and only becomes an event at some later point'.[20]

But while suggesting that a spectrum of dysfunctional behaviours may be experienced by trauma victims, theorists have also pointed to strategies by which victims seek to come to grips with its effects. Itzvan Deak refers to trauma victims retreating into 'idyllic memories of a mythicized past'.[21] Granofsky writes of a 'fragmentation' of self yielding to a phase of 'regression', which can mark either a first step towards return to 'normal' life, or a development which reinforces the trauma victim's feelings of isolation and vulnerability.[22] Salinger's post-war work fits with this pattern of regression and return. The opening section of 'For Esmé' recounts in nostalgic fashion a visit prior to the D-Day landings made by 'Sgt. X', the narrator, to a church in a Devon village where he listens to a children's choir and his encounter in a teashop with an English girl he observes in the church. Even as the story goes on to record the harrowing symptoms of combat-induced trauma, the narrative exhibits a strategy adopted as the authorial self sought to come to terms with the war; by the end of the story the narrator is on the road to recovery. The first fully articulated instance in Salinger's writing of an adolescent possessed of redemptive force, Esmé assumes her curative powers partly because of her link to an 'idyllic' episode prior to the narrator's traumatisation, partly for the poise she maintains in the face of her own overwhelming loss (her father's wartime death). Significantly, the opening, nostalgic, more intimate account – which frames the third-person 'trauma' section of the story – marks the turn to a fictional 'testimonial' form that becomes a hallmark of Salinger's post-war writing.

The retrospective tendency is mirrored more broadly in Salinger's post-war fiction, notably in *Catcher*. Having pointed to any number of parallels between the youthful Salinger's life and his protagonist's narrative, biographers would seem to confirm the view that Holden is 'a character whose curriculum vitae is in almost every detail like the author's own'.[23] In terms of settings and Holden's age, experience and social background, the novel evokes what would have been an earlier, 'simpler', pre-trauma phase of life. Enough in the novel – accounts of student antics and the tedium of dormitory life at 'Pencey Prep', tales of Manhattan nightlife, confessions about girls and sex – have the ring of truth, bolstering the autobiographical claim. But there are enough disparities between the life and

17 Granofsky, *The Trauma Novel*, p. 16.
18 Kali Tal, *Worlds of Hurt: Reading the Literature of Trauma*, Cambridge: Cambridge University Press, 1996, p. 21.
19 Caruth, *Trauma*, p. 6.
20 Anne Whitehead, *Trauma Fiction*, Edinburgh: Edinburgh University Press, 2004, p. 6.
21 Itzvan Deak, 'Memories of Hell', *The New York Review of Books*, 1997, 44, p. 38.
22 Granofsky, *The Trauma Novel*, p. 18.
23 Hamilton, *In Search of J. D. Salinger*, p. 12.

the work as to suggest other, more obscure intentions at work. There is little about the Caulfield family (with exception of an East Side residence and privileged social status) which resembles Salinger's own: Salinger had no older brother, no deceased younger brother, nor, for that matter, a younger sister – all key figures in Holden's narrative – nor does the record suggest that Salinger ever tried to run away from school. On the contrary, evidence points to Salinger having been a reasonably well-adjusted, above average student who does not seem to have caused school authorities any difficulties, nor as a young man was he ever hospitalised for psychiatric or other reasons.[24] It would, I think, be safe to say that Salinger's youth was remarkably un-Holdenish.

But if, in evoking a youthful past, the novel points to denial of the sort symptomatic of trauma, trauma-associated affects repeatedly break through the surface of a text one recent critic goes so far as to describe as 'transparently charming' and 'bereft of violence'.[25] Viewed as an instance of 'trauma fiction' – both in its expression of affects specific to trauma and its reticence in naming the sources of such affects – the narrative exhibits the manoeuvering by which the authorial self sought to work through his tormented relation to the war: both as traumatised combatant but also in the perhaps more guilt-inducing role of writer who had given enthusiastic backing to the war effort. While Salinger himself was able to resume his career with little difficulty – suggesting a degree of psychic resilience – equally clear is the self-censorship exercised with regard to his wartime experience. Whitehead has noted, however, that 'trauma does not lie in the possession of the individual to be recorded at will, but rather acts as a haunting or possessive influence which insistently and intrusively returns'.[26] Thus, even as Salinger sets about writing a novel on his preferred subject – the lives of 'young people' – the text betrays the effects of something other than a writer's recollections of adolescence. It is in such terms – a refiguring of early life in the wake of the psychically disfiguring events which subsequently transpired – that one can account for Holden's erratic, occasionally baffling behaviour. Why does a gregarious, intellectually alert, emotionally receptive young man simultaneously find himself repeatedly in the grip of catatonic despondency and suicidal bouts of depression? While Holden, always open to others and ready to respond on equal terms, displays a certain affability, he also ultimately calls the whole of society to account for some unnamed hurt, a society from which he feels compelled, in his visions of retreat to the New England woods, to escape at all costs. Referring to 'the unbearable ordeal of having to endure, absorb, to *take in* with no end and no limit', Felman characterises extreme trauma as 'unerasable and untranscendable'.[27] Incapable of forgetting, the victim finds the experience itself incommunicable – an aspect of trauma signified in Holden's narrative by the absence of explicit reference to the war – and yet everything the post-traumatic subject comes to know and see of the world is viewed through the lens of the trauma-inducing, reality-transforming event.

24 Hamilton, *In Search of J. D. Salinger*, pp. 25–31.
25 Stephen J. Whitfield, 'Cherished and Cursed: Towards a Social History of *The Catcher in the Rye*', *New England Quarterly*, 70, pp. 569–71.
26 Whitehead, *Trauma Fiction*, p. 6.
27 Shoshana Felman, 'Education and Crisis, or the Vicissitudes of Teaching', in Caruth, *Trauma*, pp. 35–6.

Thus if *Catcher* would seem to exemplify the traumatised victim's return to the pre-trauma past, that moment – adolescence and school life – is presented as anything but idyllic. For considerable stretches of the narrative, Holden is in a state of numb, near-suicidal depression. Read as exemplifying the post-war teenager's 'spiritual odyssey', an adolescent's quest for identity, or the uncertainties associated with youth in the Cold War era, it also attests to conditions – injury, illness, madness, suicide – which mark it as something more than a *Bildungsroman à l'americaine* (an American coming-of-age story).[28] Personifying, on the one hand, the affluence, mobility, spontaneity, outspokenness associated with the post-war 'teenager', Holden is for the greater part of the narrative isolated and alone, obsessed with thoughts of death and dying, fraught with fears of illness and paralysis, periodically given to outbursts of violent rage, the roots of which would seem to lie with Holden's grief over Allie, the much-loved younger brother, dead of leukaemia. Indeed, Holden is in a state of near-inconsolable mourning, his narrative repeatedly veering into elegiac recollection of the deceased sibling. In the grip of this grief, Holden becomes ever more grimly convinced of his own imminent death, an example of what Laub alludes to when he speaks of the trauma victim fearing 'that fate will strike again'.[29] Haunted by memories of Allie, alone in his dormitory room, ('so lonesome [. . .] I almost wished I was dead' [Ch. 7, p. 42]), Holden impulsively bolts, only to find himself in a Manhattan hotel room again alone and succumbing to thoughts of 'jumping out the window' (Ch. 14, p. 94). When not contemplating suicide, he is convinced that, like Allie, he is suffering a fatal illness: a 'tumor on the brain' (Ch. 8, p. 51); 'pneumonia' (Ch. 20, p. 139); 'cancer' that would have him 'dead in a couple of months' (Ch. 25, p. 176). Assaulted by Maurice the bellhop, he lies doubled up on the floor certain 'I was dying [. . .] I was drowning' (Ch. 14, p. 93), lines which momentarily betray the experience of combat, as at a later point, Holden imagines himself with a 'bullet in my guts' (Ch. 20, p. 135). Wandering about Manhattan, Holden is suddenly struck by fears of instantaneous extinction: a 'feeling that I'd never get to the other side of the street' (Ch. 25, p. 178). Felman speaks of trauma as the feeling that one is 'impotent' to act.[30] Holden here, again, feels himself powerless to affect events: 'I thought I'd just go down, [. . .] and nobody'd ever see me again' (Ch. 25, p. 178).

But if trauma theorists have underscored the aspect of regression that would seem to lie behind Salinger's evocation of a pre-trauma phase of life, they also speak of the need 'to move on' that Granofsky terms 'reunification'.[31] Thus if Holden's repeated attempts to contact former classmates and girlfriends may attest to post-war youth's orientation to the peer group, it also suggests the desire to re-establish some more 'normal' social life following his crisis and departure from Pencey Prep. A compulsive user of telephones, incessantly calling to arrange dates and make appointments, Holden experiences an obsessive need to talk. He

28 Pamela Steinle, ' "If a Body Catch a Body": *The Catcher in the Rye* Censorship Debate as Expression of Nuclear Culture', in R. Edsforth and L. Bennett (eds), *Popular Culture and Political Change in Modern America*, Albany, NY: State University of New York Press, 1991, p. 128.
29 Felman and Laub, *Testimony*, p. 67.
30 Felman, in Caruth, *Trauma*, p. 35.
31 Granofsky, *The Trauma Novel*, p. 18.

strikes up conversations with anyone who will listen – mothers of classmates, nuns, taxi drivers, tourists from Seattle, hat-check girls – and bears a special grudge against those who refuse to respond. Lack of response is a principal criteria by which he judges others: 'That's the way you can always tell a moron. They never want to discuss anything' (Ch. 6, p. 39). Priding himself on his own 'moral standards', Holden nevertheless picks up girls he meets by chance; calls the reportedly promiscuous girlfriend of a friend in hopes of a date; has a young prostitute sent to his hotel room (with whom he then only wishes to 'talk'). But virtually every exchange ends in miscommunication and ever deepening isolation. As the impossibility of communicating – and of eliciting a response – becomes ever more apparent, there occurs what Krystal, in the case of trauma victims, perceives as a 'destruction of basic trust', both in others and oneself.[32]

In a narrative fashioned around a protagonist in perpetual motion who, in the course of three days, experiences dozens of encounters, there is little sense of any forward movement or psychological development. If anything, Holden's succession of thwarted encounters propels him inexorably towards the final crisis which lands him in the California sanatorium from which he will eventually tell his story. Against the backdrop of rebuffed companionship, it is Holden's identification with his dead brother that ultimately provides the narrative's deeper continuity. Memories of Allie recur throughout the text, lending structure to Holden's narrative whilst also affirming the inescapable nature of his trauma. Clearly, none of the people that Holden meets on his journey around Manhattan can offer him the sense of connectedness he feels with his brother and every flawed encounter serves only to confirm that the loss of Allie is the central event of Holden's life. The depth of Holden's attachment to Allie is testimony to his capacity for loyalty, and to an ideal of the authentically humane, but it is also the most telling symptom of his own death-obsessed condition. Whatever consolation he finds in his evocations of the younger brother and efforts to communicate – 'I was talking to my brother Allie [. . .] don't let me disappear' (Ch. 25, p. 178) – they only underscore his own psychic fragility. If the significance of Allie's death would seem clear enough – it marks the passing of childhood, a life stage which the sixteen-year-old Holden, despite yearning for the checker-playing 'innocence' of his own childhood, recognises as irrecoverable – it can also be read as a projection of what within the subject has been 'killed off'. As brother figure, Allie is a 'double', embodying a death Holden experiences as his own. In a culminating moment, Holden sits alone at night in Central Park, rapt in a vision of himself reunited with the deceased brother. In despair, he plays out the funereal scenario: 'I felt sorry as hell for my mother and father. Especially my mother, because she still isn't over my brother Allie yet', and goes on to reflect in terms that convey both anger and morbid self-denigration on how his remains will be disposed of: 'I hope to hell when I do die somebody has sense enough to just dump me in the river' (Ch. 20, pp. 139–40). Refusal to have his death commemorated only attests to his state of sunken, blank abjection. His subsequent return to his parents' Manhattan apartment is less homecoming than final leave-taking. In a post-mortem vision of

---

32 Henry Krystal, 'Trauma and Aging: A Thirty-Year Follow-Up,' in Caruth, *Trauma*, p. 80.

himself, he imagines 'how old Phoebe would feel if I [. . .] died' (Ch. 20, p. 140). Nearing the end of his wanderings, he finds himself at the Natural History Museum, immured in a tomb in the Egyptian room, staging what is in effect a mock funeral. Having contemplated the epitaph on his tombstone, he retreats to the museum bathroom where, for reasons not altogether clear, he falls unconscious. Again stressing the proximity of death, he is certain 'I could've killed myself' (Ch. 25, p. 184).

If the victim, fixated on the trauma-inducing event, persists in feeling 'exposed' in ways which lead to a never-ending search for 'refuge' – ultimately in death itself – the condition also provokes rage, a lashing out at those perceived as responsible for the injury that has been inflicted. For those 'wounded by reality' this can, ultimately, be everyone and everything one encounters. Thus while Holden's aggression towards his room-mate (to the point of provoking Stradlater into beating him bloody) bespeaks adolescent jealousy, his subsequent outbursts are directed at an ever-expanding array of targets: the older brother who has 'prostituted' himself to the Hollywood studios; the film studios for their bogus renditions of war; writers like Hemingway who glorified violence; his school's benefactor, the undertaker Ossenburger who asks 'Jesus to send him a few more stiffs' (Ch. 3, p. 14). Holden's most pointed comments, however, are reserved for the military and those responsible for the threat of ever more cataclysmic violence. In a narrative remarkably reticent about specifying the causes of Holden's condition, it is his endorsement of his writer-brother's comments about the American military – an 'Army practically as full of bastards as the Nazis were' – and recognition of the catastrophic implications of the atomic bomb which come closest to accounting for his anger and why it is 'you got to hate everybody in the world' (Ch. 18–19, pp. 126–8). In a line where one hears the voice not of the teenager on the run, but an authorial self which has suffered the brutalising effect of combat, Holden declares: 'If there's another war, they better just take me out and stick me in front of a firing squad' (Ch. 18, p. 127). In a comment in which feelings of anger, despair and visions of mass annihilation converge, he swears: 'I'm going to sit right the hell on top of [the atomic bomb]' (Ch. 18, p. 127).

In the allusions to firing squads, atomic bombs, self-immolation and suicide, we sense not only outwardly directed rage, but a redirection of aggression onto the self. If the novel reflects a world where what Freud referred to as 'pathological mourning' has become the norm – a condition in which the depth of the subject's identification with the deceased object (both Holden with Allie and the author with an imagined earlier 'self') inhibits the working through of the subject's grief – it is here that Holden's repeatedly provocative behaviour begins to point to a deeper-lying counter-dynamic at work within the narrative. While the novel evokes a world radically at odds with what is known about Salinger's relatively uneventful years at the Valley Forge school, it is precisely this 'uneventfulness' that constitutes the more vexing issue that the authorial self seeks to come to grips with. A victim who recognises himself as 'perpetrator' of his own victimisation, Salinger comes to perceive himself as having acquiesced in an ideological system complicit in the making of a world of unspeakable horror. If the novel describes a guilt-driven death wish, it also ultimately seeks to suggest how what the authorial self had suffered might in fact have been avoided. The novel can, in this sense, be viewed less as a post-trauma effort to recapture 'lost time' than a radical rewriting of early life, prompted by profound *disavowal* of what the authorial self had been and lived through as a young man: a revision of early life which provides a measure of the guilt the authorial self had come to feel about his wartime roles. The novel, then, represents a means by which Salinger could make reparation – in the form of a message and model to readers – and thus come, in his own way, to terms with his participation in the war. In this sense, the novel seeks less to evoke an 'innocent' pre-trauma phase of life, than promote attitudes embodied in a character, Holden, who is the antithesis of what the authorial self had been.

The Holden figure can be read as a composite of voices and life stages: 'adolescent' in terms of language, age, physique, generational status; 'adult' in terms of the loss and grief he experiences; 'post-adult' in terms of his 'refusal' to accept the cataclysmic impasse to which those in authority have brought the world. However much in sympathy with adolescence, the novel is composed not from the position of 'arrested development', but from the vantage point of an 'adult' who, in going back over his own life, relives that earlier moment in terms of his subsequent life course and indicts himself for complacency and not having known better. In an early critique of *Catcher*, Leslie Fiedler was to make caustic reference to Salinger as a 'teenage impersonator'; the dismissiveness of Fiedler's comment aside, it gets at a crucial aspect of the ventriloquism that informs the Holden character.[33] Just as it would be wrong to identify the novel as an attempt to recapture a lost, 'innocent' past – the point is precisely that this past was *not* innocent – it would also be wrong to argue that *The Catcher in the Rye* is simply concerned with issues of generational difference. Ultimately, it is much more about what 'adulthood' itself has come to mean in terms of political and cultural role in a traumatised (not merely 'compromised' or 'corrupted') world for which adults continue to bear responsibility.

If Salinger has been chastised for the overtly moralising element in his fiction – what Joan Didion calls Salinger's predilection 'for giving instructions for living' – this was, in a sense, precisely the point.[34] It was an impulse which becomes more pronounced in the final sequence of Seymour Glass narratives in which Holden's diatribe against militarism has become an aggressively communicated pacifist doctrine. In *Raise High the Roof Beam, Carpenters* (1955) the horrors of war are such that even the most eloquent statements in its defense can only be condemned. Referring to nation's best-known apologia for the 'ultimate sacrifice', the narrator (Buddy Glass, yet another of the authorial self's incarnations) re-envisions the scene of Lincoln's Gettysburg address: '51,112 men were casualties at Gettysburg, and if someone *had* to speak at the anniversary of the event, he should simply have come forward and shaken his fist at his audience and then walked off – that is, if the speaker was an absolutely honest man.'[35] Salinger's silence is, I would

33 Leslie Fiedler, 'Up from Adolescence', in Henry Grunwald, *Salinger: A Critical and Personal Portrait*, New York: Harper Colophon, 1962, p. 58.
34 Joan Didion, 'Finally (Fashionably) Spurious', in Grunwald, *Salinger: A Critical and Personal Portrait*, p. 79.
35 J. D. Salinger, *Raise High the Roofbeam, Carpenters and Seymour: An Introduction*, London: Penguin, 1994, p. 46.

suggest, precisely of the sort his revisionary Lincoln ('honest Abe') has recourse to at Gettysburg – the silence of 'an absolutely honest man' in the face of hideous horror and mass suffering. It is in these terms that we might understand Salinger's silence today – a silence which continues to speak of precisely what it cannot say.

Clive Baldwin, '"Digressing from the point": Holden Caulfield's women'

Clive Baldwin has worked with the Open University in the UK since 1974. Initially developing distance-teaching courses for the Arts Faculty, he now supports innovation in the faculty's teaching and is an Open University Summer School and online course tutor. He is also a part-time research student at Birkbeck College, University of London, where he is completing his thesis, 'Representations of the Male Body and the Negotiation of Masculinity in Contemporary Fiction'. Baldwin is particularly interested in the ways in which masculinity is portrayed in post-war American fiction and the social issues that shape the construction and performance of masculinity. In this essay, he focuses on Holden's responses to the female characters in *Catcher* – which include love, admiration, desire, fear and even misogyny – and considers what those reactions reveal about Holden himself and the position of women in post-war America. Building on the material introduced in Texts and contexts (**pp. 13–16**), Baldwin discusses the ways in which post-war anxieties about the negative impact of femininity on conventional masculinity, including the 'momism' that supposedly made sheltered boys into passive men, coupled with social conventions that imposed restrictive gender roles on men and women, caused men to feel anxious about femininity, both in women and in themselves. Baldwin's essay shows how Holden's comments about the women he encounters in the novel sometimes confirm his unreliability as a narrator and suggest that his self-perception may be at odds with his performance of masculinity. Further, in Baldwin's reading, the novel itself raises doubts about the validity of conventional models of masculine behaviour by offering the reader a sympathetic hero who communicates through his actions and words, in ways both intentional and unintentional, what is problematic about a society that encourages people to behave and relate to each other in particular ways because of their gender.

Clive Baldwin, ' "Digressing from the point": Holden Caulfield's women'

> [. . .] there were about a million girls sitting and standing around waiting for their dates to show up. Girls with their legs crossed, girls with their legs not crossed, girls with terrific legs, girls with lousy legs, girls that looked like swell girls, girls that looked like they'd be bitches if you knew them. It was really nice, sightseeing [. . .].
>
> (Ch. 17, p. 111)

Holden Caulfield's description of the 'million girls' in the lobby of the Biltmore Hotel offers a reminder that *The Catcher in the Rye* contains many female characters. The novel's women have received little critical attention and this may be a result of Salinger's decision to narrate the novel in Holden's voice, thus limiting the narrative to a single, male perspective that renders the female characters marginal. In one sense, Holden's view of these women is unremarkable for an adolescent male in 1950s America: here and elsewhere he frequently echoes conventional attitudes to women that reflect women's subordination at this time. For instance, Holden's 'sightseeing' could simply be regarded as typical of an objectifying and sexualising male gaze. Furthermore, he assumes that the inevitable destination of the young women at the Biltmore is marriage (Ch. 17, p. 111). This essay, however, argues that the novel offers a more complex representation of Holden's interactions with the female characters than it might initially appear to do. For example, at the Biltmore, Holden positions himself as a sophisticated heterosexual 'man about town', and yet, while he watches and judges the young women, he is in fact identified with them: he too is sitting and waiting for his date, just as they are. The novel suggests, therefore, that Holden's image of himself as a conventional adult male is a delusion. Indeed, because he is an unreliable narrator, his perception of what is happening around him and his account of other characters cannot be trusted. Particularly in relation to the female characters, the text's continual revelation of Holden's misperceptions, inconsistencies and uncertainties creates doubt about how to interpret his attitudes to women and his descriptions of their behaviour. By focusing on two aspects of Holden's relationships with female characters – in terms of sexuality and mothering – it becomes evident that Holden is strongly identified with the feminine and the maternal. Thus, while Holden may appear to hold conventional attitudes to women, his identification with the feminine expresses an ambivalent attitude to the dominant model of masculinity.

As the title of this essay suggests, Holden's ambivalence towards the expectations of the adult male and his attraction to the feminine is metaphorically represented in his enthusiasm for 'digression'. Throughout his narrative, Holden digresses from the point in a manner that raises questions about his presentation of straightforward masculinity. He articulates his fondness for 'digression' during his conversation with his ex-English teacher, Mr Antolini. He explains that the requirement of his Oral Expression teacher at Pencey, Mr Vinson, was that speakers '*un*ify and *simpl*ify all the time' (Ch. 24, p. 166). If a speaker failed to keep to the point, the rest of the class yelled 'Digression!' (Ch. 24, p. 165).

However, Holden likes digression, which he believes is 'more *interesting*' (Ch. 24, p. 165). Vinson's view of the ideal trajectory of narrative can be characterised as conventionally rationalistic – direct, logical, purposive – traits commonly associated with masculinity. 'Digression', on the other hand, which is meandering rather than linear, fits with conventional notions of the 'feminine'. Holden's preference for digression can therefore be seen as a rejection of the rational, structured speech of male authority in preference for a more feminine mode of narration. Veering off the point is characteristic of Holden's narrative voice throughout the novel, so its form works to disrupt a simple masculine point of view. Moreover, Holden's association with the digressive and the feminine makes a significant contribution to the novel's critical relationship to masculine coming-of-age narratives. Holden tells his readers in the first sentence that he will not be going into 'all that David Copperfield kind of crap' (Ch. 1, p. 1). Unlike other male narrators of fictional biography, who look back on their adolescence from maturity, Holden remains ambiguously located at the end of the novel, associated with the feminine, and with his development into conventional adult masculinity thus still open to doubt (Ch. 26, p. 192).

The uncertainty of Holden's masculinity is reflected in his ambivalent attitude to women. Sally Hayes is one of the most prominent female characters in the novel and is one of those about whom Holden's former teacher, Antolini, asks him: 'How're all your women?' (Ch. 24, p. 171). Holden feels both attracted to and repelled by Sally: 'She gave me a pain in the ass, but she was very good-looking' (Ch. 15, p. 96). He responds to her in conventional ways, willing to engage in sexual fantasies about her, 'horse around' with her in the taxi (Ch. 17, p. 112), and admire her in her 'little blue butt-twitcher of a dress' (Ch. 17, p. 116) when they go skating. Given the expectation of marriage as a natural trajectory for young women like Sally, she might be regarded as a potential partner for Holden. He enunciates this possibility when he sees her arrive at the Biltmore, proclaiming: 'I felt like marrying her the minute I saw her' (Ch. 17, p. 112). Holden's sexual interaction with Sally is not entirely successful, however: although he believes he is 'seductive as hell' in the taxi, he almost falls off his seat twice (Ch. 17, p. 113), and the two make a clumsy couple on the ice (Ch. 17, p. 116). The implication is that Holden cannot play the role of adult partner successfully and, when he suggests running away with Sally to New England – which is partly a sexual fantasy and partly an attempt to escape the phoniness that Holden sees everywhere – she refuses. At this point, Holden's perception of her as desirable shifts and he repositions her as a judgemental mother. Geoffrey Gorer, an English social anthropologist, argued in a 1948 study that the American conscience was 'predominantly feminine', and maintained that this was problematic for the American male, who carried around inside him, 'an ethical, admonitory, censori-ous mother'.[1] With maternal concern, Sally argues that they might '*starve* to death' in New England and tells Holden that they will have 'oodles of time later' to go to 'marvelous places', once they are married (Ch. 17, p. 119). In what Holden perceives as her moralistic and restrictive reaction to his plan, Sally may

---

1   Geoffrey Gorer, *The American People: A Study in National Character*, New York: Norton, 1948, p. 54.

be deemed to be speaking as the 'censorious mother' identified by Gorer, and Holden responds with a final insult that rejects Sally and her values: 'You give me a royal pain in the ass' (Ch. 17, p. 120). While the novel slots Sally into the two dominant stereotypes of women available in 1950s America (sexual object and mother), Holden's vacillation between the two, his reluctance to see Sally simply as a sexual partner, expresses his ambivalence towards a dominant model of manhood.

While the text is sensitive to Holden's struggle to negotiate a place in the world, it simultaneously suggests that his judgement of Sally is open to question and that his representation of her should be read as both flawed and limited. All through the scenes with Sally, Holden's perspective is dominant and he presents her in an unflattering light: she is 'the queen of the phonies' (Ch. 16, p. 105), the embodiment of the inauthenticity that he is so anxious to avoid. Yet Holden's ambivalence also involves some hypocrisy: a phoniness of his own. While he thinks Sally is a 'pain in the ass', he also tells her that he loves her, while admitting that this is a lie (Ch. 17, p. 113). Moreover, his hostility towards the Ivy League 'jerk' that they meet at the theatre manifests sexual jealousy: 'He didn't *hesi*tate to horn in on my date' (Ch. 17, p. 115). He is ambivalent about Sally and yet possessive. In these ways, the text calls into question Holden's assertions about what is or is not authentic. What emerges, in fact, is an identification of Holden with Sally in terms of their social class and cultural interests. Holden's hostility towards Sally may then be read as a projection of anxiety about the authenticity of the male role to which he aspires. Moreover, Holden's inconsistent attitude and extreme behaviour, such as lighting matches (Ch. 17, p. 116) and shouting (Ch. 17, p. 117), inverts the idea that it is Sally who is the 'royal pain in the ass'. While this reassessment of the narrative does not hand Sally autonomy or genuine agency, it opens up the possibility of a more sympathetic reading of her and raises important doubts about Holden.

In other places, the narrative further exposes Holden as a problematical narrator and engages the reader's sympathy with the female characters. An example of this comes soon after Holden's arrival in New York, when he goes to the Lavender Room at the Edmont Hotel. Sitting at the table next to him are three 'girls around thirty or so. The whole three of them were pretty ugly, and they all had on the kind of hats that you knew they didn't really live in New York, but one of them, the blonde one, wasn't too bad' (Ch. 10, p. 62). Here again Holden is 'sightseeing' and he makes a number of judgements about the young women: about their physical appearance, their age and their provincialism. He names them as 'girls', thus positioning them within his imagined sexual orbit, and his behaviour from then on corresponds with this assumption. The reader may be drawn into Holden's value judgements, yet, as the episode moves on, the narrative serves to question and complicate the interchange. Holden is acting as if he is a grown-up, but he is refused an alcoholic drink because he is under-age: despite his claims about his appearance, he is obviously not an adult. It is in this light that his 'giving the three witches at the next table the eye' must be seen (Ch. 10, p. 63). Holden claims that their response was to start 'giggling like morons', but the reader might in fact begin to appreciate the young women's point of view: perhaps Holden does cut a rather absurd figure. This opens to question his assumption that he is entitled to make these sexual and class judgements about them. This is reinforced after he has been dancing with Bernice and he sits down with the women, even though, he says, they 'didn't invite me to sit down at their table – mostly because they were too ignorant' (Ch. 10, p. 65). Holden here draws on the codes of conventional male behaviour in imposing himself uninvited on the space occupied by the women, but it is clear that it is his behaviour rather than theirs that is 'ignorant'. The representation of Holden's exchange with these young women is therefore complex. It could be read as a critique of his rather boorish attitudes and behaviour, yet these might be considered broadly consistent with that of an adult male in contemporary New York society, a status to which he aspires. His failure to be considered an adult is partly a consequence of his adolescent limitations, but his conduct also implies a more fundamental question about whether the masculinity for which he strives is itself flawed.

As the scene in the Lavender Room unfolds, Holden's attempt to perform the conventional male role is undercut by his identification with the women. He may be depressed by the news that they will get up early to see the first show at the Radio City Music Hall, but later he too visits Radio City and it is evident that, like the women, he is vulnerable and marginalised in New York. Holden perceives himself as a Manhattan insider: he knows, for example, that movie stars will not come to the Lavender Room (Ch. 10, p. 66). Yet, because he is lacking the authority of the adult male, he too is compromised as an autonomous agent, and, as the narrative unfolds, his helplessness and frailty are increasingly exposed. The identification of Holden with these young women therefore connects him to the feminine. By associating Holden with female characters, the novel questions conventional notions of masculinity and expresses his ambivalence to the male world of work and responsibility.

Through its representation of Holden's attitude to masculinity, the narrative deconstructs normative expectations of male sexuality. Critics have often interpreted Holden's resistance to sexual contact as his clinging to innocence, but it could alternatively be seen as evidence of his resistance to heterosexual ideals. This may be seen in the examples of the characters of Sunny and Jane. According to 1950s middle-class moral codes, sex should be constrained, particularly because pregnancy outside marriage provoked severe disapproval. Abortion and birth control were not accessible, so the answer was 'petting', which required complete control of the boundaries of sexual contact to avoid pregnancy. This control was the responsibility of the girl: 'The boy is expected to ask for as much as possible, the girl to yield as little as possible.'[2] The allocation of control to the 'girl' implies that the female has no desire of her own, other than to control her partner, thus denying the possibility of active female sexuality. As Holden states, a girl who isn't a prostitute 'keeps telling you to stop' (Ch. 13, p. 83). Although he knows that when asked to stop, 'most guys don't', Holden does (Ch. 13, p. 83). Moreover, somewhat apologetically, he admits that he 'can never get really sexy – I mean *really* sexy – with a girl I don't like a lot' (Ch. 19, p. 133). This attitude is contrasted with that of Holden's roommate at Pencey, Stradlater, who is sexually aggressive and unscrupulous:

2   Margaret Mead, *Male and Female. A Study of the Sexes in a Changing World*. London: Victor Gollancz, 1949, p. 290.

What a technique that guy had. What he'd do was, he'd start snowing his date in this very quiet, *sincere* voice – like as if he wasn't only a very handsome guy, but a nice *sincere* guy, too. [. . .] His date kept saying, 'No – *please*. Please, don't. *Please*.' But old Stradlater kept snowing her in this Abraham Lincoln, sincere voice, and finally there'd be this terrific silence in the back of the car.

(Ch. 7, pp. 43–4)

In this anecdote, Holden is clearly torn between admiration for Stradlater's technique and disgust with his refusal to adhere to the boundaries of petting. The image of 'Caulfield and his Magic Violin' (Ch. 13, p. 84) suggests that, like Stradlater, Holden is caught up in the dominant discourse of female sexual passivity in which a woman is merely an instrument upon which a man may demonstrate his sexual skills. Yet in other respects he aligns himself with female sexuality. Not only does his sexual desire require an emotional dimension, in marked contrast with Stradlater's single-minded determination, Holden's preparedness to stop when asked has the additional effect of protecting his confessed virginity (Ch. 13, p. 83).

The social and moral codes involved in middle-class sexual exchanges do not apply in Holden's episode with Sunny, who is a prostitute and therefore will not say 'no'. Holden's avoidance of sex with her may be read as consistent with his need to combine sexual contact with emotional connection. The key moment occurs when Sunny unexpectedly removes her dress. This sudden transformation reveals the true nature of the circumstances those in which her body becomes an object in a financial transaction. His despair at the lack of emotional contact is reinforced by his identification with her: 'She was around my age' (Ch. 13, p. 85). They are further connected in their nervous youthfulness: Holden describes her as 'a nervous girl' and notes of himself, 'Boy, was I getting nervous' (Ch. 13, pp. 86 and 87). In a typically digressive manoeuvre, Holden tries to engage Sunny in a conversation and her resistance to this emphasises the limits of their relationship. It is finally clear that he cannot proceed when he thinks about her buying the dress. He begins to empathise with her and feel sympathy for the lack of ordinariness in her life: this identification means that he must refuse the emotionless sexual contact that prostitution offers.

Holden's identification with women is repeated in the representation of Jane Gallagher, who belongs to the same social stratum and is first mentioned when he hears that Stradlater has a date with her. Until this moment, Holden admires Stradlater's sexual prowess. However, he expresses concern for Jane through his use of the checkers metaphor. Recalling the games he played with Jane the previous summer, Holden is reminded that she 'wouldn't move any of her kings', which she kept in the back row (Ch. 4, p. 27). This signifies an unwillingness to take risks and, attempting to warn Jane against Stradlater, Holden tells his friend to ask her 'if she still keeps all her kings in the back row' (Ch. 4, p. 29), implying she should remain guarded.

In their markedly different responses to Jane, the narrative contrasts Holden and Stradlater. Stradlater's approach to sex, genitally focused and emotionally disengaged, typifies dominant notions of masculine sexuality: lust that must be satisfied, disconnected from affection. Unlike Stradlater's phallic obsession,

Holden's summer relationship with Jane, characterised by companionship, hand-holding and Jane's stroking of Holden's neck, is represented as touching and sensuous, polymorphous in its engagement of multiple areas of the body. This difference may again be considered in terms of digression. The trajectory of Stradlater's sexuality is unified and simplified in its objective: it is a sexuality that exploits discrepancies of power in contemporary gender relations. In contrast, Holden is hesitant. Not only does he not go to see Jane when she is at Pencey, throughout his time in New York, the reader is teased with the prospect of Holden speaking to her on the phone, but he either defers the call or fails to make contact, perhaps to avoid a definitive answer to the question of Jane's relationship with Stradlater. In the sharp distinction between Stradlater and Holden and Holden's empathy with Jane, he is identified with the feminine. Such identification is suffused with an ambiguity about sexuality and its relationship with gender that is disruptive of conventional expectations. It is not that Holden simply identifies with a conventional notion of female sexuality, but rather that his distance from a crude masculine phallic sexuality throws open to question the stereotypes associated with femininity and masculinity.

In addition to deconstructing male sexuality through Holden's identification with the female characters, *Catcher* is also disruptive of gender roles in its representation of the maternal. Holden's connection with mothering is twofold: he both seeks out maternal women and manifests maternal impulses himself. Reading the novel in the light of D. W. Winnicott's psychoanalytic notion of 'holding' and maternal care allows the central metaphors of the novel – falling and catching – to be read in relation to mothering.[3] Winnicott (1896–1971) was a British psychoanalyst whose post-war writings on infant development reflected the focus on the child–mother relationship central to psychoanalytic work of the period.[4] Winnicott argued that the period of infant care before the infant developed a sense of himself or herself was critical to psychic development. In this stage the child was dependent on the mother and Winnicott names this as the 'holding' stage.[5] For Winnicott, '[h]olding includes especially the physical holding of the infant which is a form of loving'.[6] *Catcher* presents a series of images and events connected to falling and catching: Allie's death and his baseball catcher's mitt; the little boy risking the traffic as he walks along singing Burns's song; the suicidal fall of James Castle; Holden's own sense of falling and disappearing. Winnicott's emphasis on holding in relation to maternal care is useful in that it reveals that Holden's desire to 'catch' (hold) others and be saved from falling himself can be understood in terms of his desire to mother and be mothered.

Indeed, from its opening dedication to Salinger's own mother, the novel continually returns to the archetype of the mother in its representation of female characters. This is perhaps not surprising given an obsession with the 'mother' in

3   I am indebted to Dr Edith Frampton for introducing me to Winnicott's notion of 'holding'.
4   For a discussion of developments in psychoanalytic theory in relation to infant development, see Eli Zaretsky, *Secrets of the Soul: A Social and Cultural History of Psychoanalysis*, New York: Knopf, 2004, Ch. 10.
5   D. W. Winnicott, 'The Theory of the Parent-Infant Relationship' (1960) in *The Maturational Processes and the Facilitating Environment: Studies in the Theory of Emotional Development*, London: Hogarth Press, 1979, pp. 37–55.
6   Winnicott, 'The Theory of the Parent-Infant Relationship', p. 49.

other contemporary discourses, much of it markedly controlling and misogyn-istic. Perhaps none was more remarkable than Philip Wylie's *Generation of Vipers* (1942), which became notorious for its introduction of the concept of 'momism'.[7] Wylie's notion of momism suggested that American women had persuaded men of the extraordinary value of mothers, turning this validation into a form of ideology. He asserts that 'megaloid mom worship has got completely out of hand. Our land, subjectively mapped, would have more silver cords and apron strings crisscrossing it than railroads and telephone wires. Mom is everywhere and everything and damned near everybody.'[8]

As a consequence, for Wylie, America was a 'matriarchy in fact if not in declar-ation'.[9] In *Their Mothers' Sons* (1946), Edward A. Strecker argues that when young men 'failed' the test of maturity when faced with combat, 'in the vast majority of case histories, a "mom" is at fault'.[10] Wylie's and Strecker's views foreground the hostility towards women in 1950s America, and in particular on the demand that women be restricted to the domestic sphere.

Such hostility to women is also evident in popular attitudes to female sexuality derived from psychoanalytic theory. For example, in Ferdinand Lundberg and Marynia Farnham's *Modern Woman: The Lost Sex* (1947) it is claimed that 'for the sex act to be fully satisfactory to a woman she must, in the depths of her mind, desire deeply and utterly, to be a mother'.[11] Such claims demonstrate the ways in which Freudian psychoanalytic theory, with its emphasis on vaginal intercourse, was coopted into conservative discourses about women's natural role as mothers, promoting the idea that, for women, sex should be for procreation rather than pleasure. The contradictions and confusions of contemporary discourses about female sexuality and mothering affect Holden's approach to women. When he meets Mrs Morrow on the train he regards her as a woman who was 'very good-looking' with 'quite a lot of sex appeal' (Ch. 8, pp. 48 and 49) and he tries to relate to her as an adult, rather flirtatiously offering her a cigarette and trying to buy her a drink. This performance is continually undercut by Mrs Morrow's maternal attitude and her repeated use of 'dear' when addressing Holden. So Holden fails to establish an erotic connection with her and comes to relate to Mrs Morrow as maternal rather than sexual. Mrs Morrow is the mother of another boy at Pencey and Holden's lies about her son are driven by his assump-tion that mothers are deluded about their children: 'Mothers are all slightly insane' (Ch. 8, p. 49). Here Holden seems to articulate an anxiety about his own inadequacies as a son and in boosting Ernest is able to bask at one remove in Mrs Morrow's motherly pride. He is prepared to tell substantial lies to hold her attention, not least his invented illness, which demands from Mrs Morrow exactly the sympathy that will be lacking when his own mother discovers the truth. Thus, Holden's projection onto Mrs Morrow of an idealised mother–son relationship articulates his craving to be mothered.

7 Philip Wylie, *Generation of Vipers*, New York: Farrar & Rinehart, 1942.
8 Wylie, *Generation of Vipers*, p. 185.
9 Wylie, *Generation of Vipers*, p. 50.
10 Edward A. Strecker, *Their Mothers' Sons: The Psychiatrist Examines an American Problem*, Philadelphia, Pa.: J. B. Lippincott, 1946, pp. 23–4.
11 Quoted in Jane Gerhard, *Desiring Revolution: Second-Wave Feminism and the Rewriting of American Sexual Thought, 1920 to 1982*, New York: Columbia University Press, 2001, p. 45.

The nuns, to whom Holden talks at Grand Central Station, do not fit either the maternal or sexual roles expected of American women. He describes the English teacher as asexual: she has 'a helluva kind face' (Ch. 15, p. 99). Holden tries to negotiate the confusion that the nuns' status as neither mothers nor sexual beings causes him: he wonders about their sexual identity in relation to reading 'books with lovers and all in them' (Ch. 15, p. 99) while at the same time the English teacher reminds him of Mrs Morrow (Ch. 15, p. 101), whom he found both sexually attractive and reassuringly maternal. In his donation to the nuns' collection, it seems that Holden again aspires to the role of the good son. Yet, when he blows smoke in the nuns' faces, an accident he considers 'very stupid and embarrassing' (Ch. 15, p. 102), he is clearly unsettled. In losing control of his cigarette smoke, Holden reveals that he is not in control of himself, suggesting that women who do not fit into the limited roles available threaten the model of masculinity he imitates.

While Holden attempts to position some of the women he meets in the role of mother – a reflection of his emotional neediness – his own mother is merely a shadowy presence in the novel. This absence may partly account for Holden's need to seek the maternal in other women. Early in the novel when Holden is 'horsing' about with Robert Ackley at Pencey, he pulls down his new hunting hat over his eyes and pretends to be blind: 'Mother darling, everything's getting so *dark* in here'; 'Mother darling, give me your *hand*. Why won't you give me your *hand*?' (Ch. 3, p. 18). Although presented playfully, Holden is expressing a desire to reach out to his mother. His closest contact with his mother comes near the end of the novel when he secretly visits Phoebe and hides in the cupboard when his parents arrive home unexpectedly. Here he is literally in the dark and the cupboard may be read as a womb-like symbol of the maternal.

However, Holden's desire to be mothered is complicated by his identification with his mother. He only describes her briefly, usually referring to her anxious disposition and on one occasion describing her as 'very hysterical' (Ch. 7, p. 45). Although 'hysteria' is a condition traditionally associated with women, Holden also manifests 'hysterical' symptoms in relation to Allie's death, breaking all the windows in the garage (Ch. 5, p. 34). Such similarities align Holden with his mother. Holden's family name also connects him to the maternal in a way that challenges the gender roles outlined in contemporary discourses that encouraged men to break away from the maternal and see women as sexual objects. Critics have pointed out that while Holden begins his story by disassociating himself from 'biographical' fiction such as *David Copperfield* (1849–50), his name and other aspects of *The Catcher in the Rye* in fact connect him to Charles Dickens's novel, first, in the 'field' that Caul*field* and Copper*field* share, but also in the 'caul', which is a membrane from the womb which sometimes covers a baby's head when it is born.[12] David Copperfield tells us that he was born with a caul, which is considered to be a sign of good luck.[13] I suggest, however, that Holden's 'caul' may more importantly signify his connection to the maternal.

12 See Robert F. Fleissner, 'Salinger's Caulfield: A Refraction of Copperfield and His Caul', in *Names, Titles, and Characters by Literary Writers: Shakespeare, 19th- and 20th-century Authors*. Studies in Onomastics, Vol. II. Lewiston, NY: Edwin Mellen Press, 2001, pp. 177–80.
13 Charles Dickens, *David Copperfield*, London and Glasgow: Collins, n.d., p. 7.

Phoebe also plays a maternal role in relation to Holden. Although only ten years old, the representation of Phoebe anticipates her adult female role. For example, when she is even younger she goes out walking with Holden and Allie, dressed in white gloves, 'like a lady and all' (Ch. 10, p. 61). Holden also attributes to his little sister an ability to make adult discriminations of taste: he notes her preference for the film *The 39 Steps* (Ch. 10, p. 61) and is confident that she will appreciate the 'Little Shirley Beans' record he buys for her (Ch. 16, pp. 104–5). Projecting onto Phoebe an adult persona means that she can be allocated the role of Holden's conscience, a responsibility often imposed on women and mothers. Consequently, it is Phoebe's judgement of Holden that makes him feel most uncomfortable when she has established that he has been expelled from Pencey (Ch. 22, pp. 150–1). Phoebe also provides motherly comfort when Holden breaks down immediately after having hidden in the cupboard (Ch. 23, pp. 161–2). Furthermore, Phoebe takes an adult role when she provides Holden with money and places her arm around his neck, metaphorically offering him the reassuring hand he called for from his mother when he was fooling around with Ackley.

However, if Phoebe's maternal relationship with Holden seems merely to affirm gender conventions, her interaction with her brother also reveals Holden's own maternal impulses. Like a mother, he feels 'swell' and contented for the first time in the novel when he sits watching her sleep (Ch. 21, p. 144). Phoebe's questions about Holden's career plans (suggesting conventional male roles such as scientist and lawyer) lead Holden to overtly reject traditional masculinity in favour of being 'the catcher in the rye' (Ch. 22, pp. 155–6). In his adaptation of Burns's song, changing the word 'meet' to 'catch', Holden replaces the sexual overtones of the original with an image of maternal care and protection. In imagining himself catching the children and preventing them from falling Holden is identified with a maternal role that closely parallels Winnicott's notion of holding: an identification that is echoed in his first name. In actively connecting Holden with maternal care, the novel subversively disconnects the pervasive equation of the female with the maternal in a manner that destabilises the novel's otherwise predictable understanding of women as the only permissible source of comfort and compassion.

In conclusion, a focus on female characters in *The Catcher in the Rye* reveals a persistent association of Holden with the feminine and the maternal that runs counter to his often conventional and sometimes misogynistic responses to women. The novel's subtle alignment of Holden with the female characters is a significant element in its critical relationship to the tradition of masculine coming-of-age narratives because it questions the protagonist's desire to mature into the conventional male role. Holden's 'digressions' challenge the phallically oriented model of male sexuality that dominated post-war America. His unspoken and unrealised identification with the feminine and maternal thus offers a subtextual critique of contemporary discourses about gender and sexuality.

4

Further reading and web resources

Further reading

Fiction by J. D. Salinger

J. D. Salinger, *Nine Stories* (Boston, Mass.: Little, Brown, 1953). Also published as *For Esmé – with Love and Squalor, and Other Stories* (London: Hamish Hamilton, 1953).
J. D. Salinger, *Franny and Zooey* (Boston, Mass.: Little, Brown, 1961).
J. D. Salinger, *Raise High the Roof Beam, Carpenters, and Seymour: An Introduction* (Boston: Little, Brown, 1963).

Salinger has published very little fiction, but anyone who likes *Catcher* will enjoy his short (and long) stories and see in them stylistic links to *Catcher*. *Nine Stories*, which includes 'For Esmé – With Love and Squalor' and 'A Perfect Day for Bananafish', is the best place to start.

Biographies of J. D. Salinger

Ian Hamilton, *In Search of J. D. Salinger* (London: Bloomsbury, 1998). Salinger took legal action to stop Hamilton publishing private letters in his biography of the author, so Hamilton wrote a book about the difficulties of writing a book about Salinger, including some interesting biographical material in the process.
Paul Alexander, *Salinger: A Biography* (Los Angeles, Calif.: Renaissance Books, 1999). Alexander used material that Hamilton had uncovered, and new documents, to produce the only conventional biography of Salinger to date. It received a mixed reaction from critics, but is an interesting book.

Post-war America

George Brown Tindall and David E. Shi, *America: A Narrative History*, 4th edn (New York: Norton, 1996). A clear introductory guide to American history, wide-ranging but including plenty of useful information about the post-war period.

William H. Chafe, *The Unfinished Journey: America Since World War II* (Oxford: Oxford University Press, 2003). An excellent alternative to Tindall (and more focused on *Catcher*'s era) this is detailed and interesting: the standard work on post-war America.

Lary May (ed.), *Recasting America: Culture and Politics in the Age of Cold War* (Chicago, Ill.: Chicago University Press, 1989). Also more period-specific, this collection of essays is especially recommended for its lively analyses of the culture of the period.

Peter Biskind, *Seeing is Believing* (New York: Henry Holt, 1983; London: Bloomsbury, 2001). A fascinating exploration of Hollywood films of the 1950s, analysing the ways in which they respond to the politics and society of post-war America.

Elaine Tyler May, *Homeward Bound: American Families in the Cold War Era* (New York: Basic Books, 1999). This key study includes material on the impact of the Depression and the war on the family, as well as on issues such as sex, gender roles and the 'baby boom'.

Studies of *The Catcher in the Rye*

Marvin Laser and Norman Fruman (eds), *Studies in J. D. Salinger: Reviews, Essays, and Critiques of The Catcher in the Rye and Other Fiction* (New York: Odyssey Press, 1963). One of the earliest anthologies of criticism, this is principally focused on *Catcher* and includes early reviews and essays from the first wave of responses to the novel; a selection of these is discussed in Critical history (**pp. 37–40**).

Henry Anatole Grunwald (ed.), *Salinger: A Critical and Personal Portrait* (New York: Harper Colophon, 1962). This includes extracts from the early essays that compare Holden to Huckleberry Finn and a substantial section from Donald Costello's analysis of language in *Catcher* (see also Critical history, **pp. 40–4**).

Joel Salzberg (ed.), *Critical Essays on Salinger's The Catcher in the Rye* (Boston, Mass.: G. K. Hall, 1990). This anthology includes early reviews, a few 'classic' essays and four new readings, including those by Mellard and Schriber discussed in Critical history (**pp. 60–3**).

Harold Bloom (ed.), *Holden Caulfield* (Philadelphia, Pa.: Chelsea House, 1990). This collection of extracts from reviews and essays will be most useful if the books listed above prove difficult to locate.

Jack Salzman (ed.), *New Essays on The Catcher in the Rye* (Cambridge: Cambridge University Press, 1991) and J. P. Steed (ed.), *The Catcher in the Rye: New Essays* (New York: Peter Lang, 2002). There is interesting material in both of these collections of new essays on *Catcher* (neither collection contains an overview of the novel or a critical history). Christopher Brookeman's essay 'Pencey Preppy' (in Salzman) on the significance of the prep school in *Catcher* and Robert Miltner's 'Mentor Mori' (in Steed) about peer group society and Holden's search for a role model are certainly worthwhile.

Morris Dickstein, *Leopards in the Temple: The Transformation of American Fiction 1945–1970* (Cambridge, Mass.: Harvard University Press, 2002).

Discusses *Catcher* and other fiction of the same period; a very useful book for anyone interested in the work of Salinger and his contemporaries, including Norman Mailer, Ralph Ellison and Jack Kerouac.

Adolescence

Thomas Hine, *The Rise and Fall of the American Teenager* (New York: Perennial, 2000). An engaging, clear and wide-ranging history of the ways in which adolescence has been understood in the USA.

Neil Campbell (ed.), *American Youth Cultures* (Edinburgh: Edinburgh University Press, 2004). A collection of essays on a range of fiction related to American youth; no essay specifically on *Catcher* but a good resource for those wishing to expand their reading in this field.

Web-based resources

'Featured Author: J. D. Salinger', *The New York Times on the Web*, <http://www.nytimes.com/books/98/09/13/specials/salinger.html>. A valuable selection of reviews and articles about Salinger from the archive of *The New York Times*.

'Investigating *The Catcher in the Rye*', <http://www.umsl.edu/~gryan/amer.studies/amst.catcherwegquest.html>. This web site, created by the American Studies department at the University of Missouri–St. Louis, contains many useful links to Salinger and *Catcher*-related resources.

'The Literature and Culture of the American 1950s', <http://www-.writing.upenn.edu/~afilreis/50s/home.html>. An impressive web site created by the University of Pennsylvania. Contains hundreds of links to a range of material including reproduced documents of the era, essays on key figures, images, interviews and speeches.

'*The Catcher in the Rye* Pages', <http://www.euronet.nl/users/los/tcitr.html>. A well-produced and long-running web site created by a *Catcher* enthusiast: a good starting point.

'*The Catcher in the Rye* and Related Matters', <http://www.wahlbrinck.de/catcherintherye/index.htm>. Another useful web site created by an admirer of the novel which offers some interesting connections to other texts.

'Dead Caulfields', <http://www.geocities.com/deadcaulfields/DCHome.html>. Contains information on Salinger's early writing as well as on *Catcher*. A well-organised and nicely presented site with helpful material.

Index